WHAT'S BEST FOR THE BODY?

Pastoral Transitions in the Local Church

DAVID CULVER

WESTBOW
PRESS®
A DIVISION OF THOMAS NELSON
& ZONDERVAN

WestBow Press books may be ordered through booksellers or by contacting:

WestBow Press
A Division of Thomas Nelson & Zondervan
1663 Liberty Drive
Bloomington, IN 47403
www.westbowpress.com
844-714-3454

ISBN: 978-1-6642-5693-4 (sc)
ISBN: 978-1-6642-5695-8 (hc)
ISBN: 978-1-6642-5694-1 (e)

Library of Congress Control Number: 2022902325

Print information available on the last page.

WestBow Press rev. date: 03/29/2022

To Carolyn, my "strong one."

Over forty-two years of pastoral ministry could not have happened without my wife and ministry partner, Carolyn, alongside of me. She experienced all the changes and transitions that spanned four local church pastorates in three different states. But in many respects, she was more personally affected by the transitions than I. Four times, she was uprooted from her home, her church family, and her friends to follow me to another ministry where she established another home, experienced a new church family, and built new relationships and friendships. *Carolyn* means "strong one," and she has lived up to that name, showing exemplary strength of character and remarkable emotional and spiritual fortitude. This book is dedicated to Carolyn, my God-given helper, fit for me and our ministry.

ACKNOWLEDGMENTS

Were it not for those who were and are the members of the four local churches I had the privilege of pastoring, this book would not have been written. I wish to acknowledge the saints both in heaven and on earth of Calvary Baptist Church in Delaware, Ohio; Calvary Baptist Church in Wisconsin Rapids, Wisconsin; Heritage Baptist Church in Clarks Summit, Pennsylvania; and Shawnee Hills Baptist Church in Jamestown, Ohio. They were an integral part of the transitions detailed in this book. I also wish to express my gratitude to Dr. Jeremy Pierre of Southern Seminary in Louisville, Kentucky who encouraged to me to write this book. Also, to Dave Weinerth, Chuck Pausley, and David Kisner, beloved brothers in Christ who critiqued the manuscript prior to it being submitted for publication. Finally, my deep appreciation to my wife, Carolyn, for her grammatical expertise, careful proofreading, and skillful coaching in our marriage and ministry, and with this manuscript.

CONTENTS

INTRODUCTION

"I'll never do it like that again." That was my vow after following a traditional model for leaving one pastorate for another. It was my first experience with considering a move from one local church to another, and I only knew one model: visit the other church under the pretense of being out of town (since it was out of state). So, I did it that way.

First, I met with the pastoral search committee of the new church one weekend and, two months later, I returned and candidated. That second visit was the week before Thanksgiving, so I let those of the congregation I was already pastoring think we were on vacation without ever disclosing the real reason for my absence. The rationale was that if things didn't work out, no one would need to know, and no one would be affected. And if they knew, they might want me to leave sooner than later. Well, the result of candidating was that I received a unanimous call to come as the new church's pastor. My wife and I and our four elementary-age children gave a hearty *yes* to that church's call. But then we had to tell our current church family that we were leaving them. That was hard!

I'll never forget how deceitful the whole process seemed and how unfaithful I felt to the church I had pastored for nearly eleven years. Understandably, some of them felt betrayed and others were hurt. None of them knew ahead of time, including the leadership, which heightened the sense of betrayal. The whole decision was made apart from their awareness or involvement. But that was the way it was done: secretly, with the unsuspecting church family left in shock when they were told their pastor was leaving them for another church. It was then that I determined never to do it like that again, should a similar situation arise. It did, and I didn't. I knew there had to be a better and more biblical way. There was.

Ten years later, another church approached me about being its pastor. Initially, I deflected their interest, as I had no valid reason to leave and many good reasons to stay. I did, however, agree to pray about it. After several weeks of praying, my wife and I agreed to take another step in that direction, though our strategy was to convince the other church about why we couldn't come. We actually wrote a list, "Ten Reasons Why We Can't Leave," which included: 1) a daughter who was a high school senior, and we wouldn't move during her senior year; and 2) a new church planted by our current church, and I wouldn't leave until it had a pastor. The other eight reasons seemed just as convincing, and we were confident this was an ironclad plan for why we couldn't leave.

But in a very unexpected way, the Lord began arranging our lives in such a way that we sensed he was positioning us for another change of ministry. One by one, God crossed off our reasons for not leaving. When the last one was crossed off our list (i.e., they were willing to wait for our daughter to graduate), we could no longer deny that God was up to something. But we kept praying before making any decisions or telling anyone about it.

When the time came for others to know, we did everything differently than what we had done previously. First, I informed the pastoral staff and deacons about the other church's inquiry and our interest, and we began praying together. Soon after, we told our church family, asking them to pray for us to know what to do. I remember saying to them on a Sunday evening, "For the past ten years, you have come to Carolyn and me asking for prayer over what to do about critical issues and about how to know God's will on vital decisions. Now, we're asking you to pray for us as we face a situation that we did not seek but that may be God's will." Though surprised, the church family assured us of their prayerful support.

Over the next several weeks, we and the church body prayed

about what to do. Ultimately, there was consensus within our church family that we should take the next step with the other church to gain clarity on God's will for us and the two churches involved. We accepted the invitation to candidate and our current church family gave us their blessing, promising to keep praying for us and the other church. A month after I candidated, we knew we were meant to go—as did our church family. I'll never forget one member saying, "Pastor, we don't want you to leave, but for you to stay would be disobedient." There was no sense of deceit or betrayal on either side. Our transparency and the inclusion of those we loved and who loved and prayed for us only cultivated unanimity and mutual support. When we said yes to the other church and told our current church family, their response was, "We already knew you were going. It's the right thing to do. God has answered our prayers." It was a beautiful process that God orchestrated and blessed.

Several months ensued before we moved, but I remember standing before that church family on a Sunday evening with the two associate pastors on either side of me. I put my arms around them and commended them to the church as their pastors to lead and care for them in the days ahead. Furthermore, it was my recommendation that the man I had mentored for six years, first as an intern and then as an associate, be considered as their next lead pastor. Although I couldn't make that decision for them, I wanted them to know that this man had been mentored by me and was ready, should that be God's will. By the grace of God and his providence, that associate pastor did follow me as the lead pastor. Though it was not a seamless transition, it was relatively peaceful with good consensus. The church grew and moved forward under his pastoral leadership and care. He had gifts and strengths I didn't have that were used by the Lord to expand the ministries of that local church. I recall saying to my wife about that transitional process, "This is how it ought to be done. This is a much better way. Should a similar situation arise in the future, this is the preferred process." It did.

Nine years later, we were faced with the opportunity to lead a mission agency, which meant leaving our church family and pastoral ministry. As we had done nine years earlier, we informed the leadership and our church family early in the process, asking them to pray for all of us to know God's will. I remember a church member saying, "If it's the Lord's will for you to stay here, we look forward to twenty more years of you as our pastor. But if it's his will for you to go and lead that mission, then we will send you out to serve in that capacity." A ministry of mutual intercession went on for several months until it become clear to us and our church family that we were to leave. On a memorable Sunday evening, our church commissioned us and sent us out as missionaries to administrate a mission agency as president and wife. When we left to serve Christ on a more global level, there was blessed oneness and mutual affection. How sweet it was!

Three years later, God called us to our fourth and final pastoral ministry as the lead pastor. But it was also an invitation to mentor and train the associate pastor to follow me. Thus, for seven years, I trained the associate and prepared the church for him to be the next lead pastor. I respect and admire a local church with this kind of foresight, vision, and wisdom to minimize the challenges of a pastoral transition. It was a privilege serving with those who had that visionary mindset. Although the transition of the associate pastor to lead, and me to associate, was never presented as a "done deal" to the church family, from the beginning it was shared as a preferred plan for pastoral succession. That proved to be true as through a constitutionally compliant pastoral search process, customized to our situation, the associate was called as the next lead pastor, and I was approved as the associate pastor. This, too, was a beautiful thing blessed by God. I served as a full-time associate pastor for more than a year before going part-time. Then I retired at the age of seventy, a year and a half after the transition. There was never any doubt that the transitional process we followed was Spirit-led and was best for that local body of believers.

This book is based on the true story of pastoral leadership

transitions of which I was a part. Although it is my story, I neither own it nor pretend to be the one who originated it. God did this, and I had the privilege of living it and now writing about it. So, I share this story with the hope that it will help other pastors, church leaders, and church congregations in their pastoral leadership searches and transitions. Change happens in local churches. That's a given. But it doesn't always happen well. My experience has taught me that change involving pastoral transitions can happen better than it does in most churches. And although I am not proposing a one-size-fits-all model, I believe that what I have learned can be applied to many other local churches, Baptist or otherwise.

This story has been over forty years in the making, and I am sure there will be more to share subsequent to this book. Each chapter represents the progressive unfolding of this story, beginning with my first pastoral change, thirty years ago, and ending with the most-recent transition in which I became an associate pastor having mentored a man to become the lead pastor. It is a story worth telling and one that I hope will be embraced and told by others who follow this proposed pastoral transition model.

In addition to the ten chapters, there are four appendices. Appendix A is the rest of the story in which a true story of how God prepares for future transitions is told. Appendix B consists of the three sermons I preached in a series on transitions and change based around Joshua 1. The leadership transition from Moses to Joshua is a biblical template for leadership transitions of different sorts, including pastoral. Appendix C, 3M CommUnity, is a sermon based on Philippians 2:1–5 that I preached the Sunday before the ballots were cast for the associate pastor to become the next lead pastor. Although it was meant to have been an impassioned plea for unity amid change, COVID-19 caused us to suspend in-person worship services during that time. Thus, it was prerecorded with me preaching to a camera in an empty room. It was not what I had hoped it would be, but the Lord used it to prepare hearts. Appendix D is the message I preached on my last Sunday as lead pastor and shares lessons learned in over forty years as a lead pastor. I include the last three appendices to demonstrate my pulpit ministry in the final months before the actual transition took place. I highly recommend that the lead pastor being transitioned give much prayer and preparation to preaching "last" messages that really connect with the people and speak to what they're experiencing to which the Bible clearly speaks and illustrates.

Admittedly, the *last* chapter in this story has not been written. It's a fluid, not static, process. My hope is that this book will encourage other churches to consider this model of pastoral transition that makes change more palatable and navigable. I am confident that there are other good practices in place that need to be shared that will support and complement what is in this book. In that sense, it is a work in progress. Although I believe this is a better way, an even better way is likely yet to come.

For those pastors and local churches anticipating or experiencing a transition in pastoral leadership, or for any pastor or church wondering if there is a better way to navigate this kind of change, this book proposes one. The tried-and-not-so-true traditional method may be what's familiar, but is it what's best for the body? We do well to remember Moses's words to the people of Israel in anticipation of Joshua succeeding him as their leader: "It is the LORD who goes before you. He will be with you; he will not leave you or forsake you. Do not fear or be dismayed" (Deuteronomy 31:8; unless otherwise noted, all scriptures are quoted from the English Standard Version). What encouraging words for a person or a church facing a pastoral transition. We never go it alone or find ourselves at a loss for leadership and guidance. We need not ever fear or feel hopeless. The Lord is ahead of us and with us. He will not leave us or abandon us. What security we have amid change, knowing that God's got this!

WHAT'S BEST FOR THE BODY?

(A Philosophy of Pastoral Ministry)

How believers steward their physical bodies matters to God since each believer's body is the temple of the Holy Spirit (1 Corinthians 6:19–20). The word translated as *temple* refers to the Holy of Holies or the most sanctified place in the Old Testament temple, where only the high priest was allowed to enter—once a year—to make atonement for the people. It mattered greatly to God how his people treated that most-holy sanctuary. Thus, it matters greatly to God how individual believers treat their bodies since they are the dwelling place of the Holy Spirit.

In 1 Corinthians 3:16–17, Paul writes to the body of believers in Corinth, "Do you not know that you are God's temple and that God's Spirit dwells in you? If anyone destroys God's temple, God will destroy him. For God's temple is holy, and you are that temple." The *you* in these verses is plural, referring to all who were and are part of the body of Christ, from the first century AD in Corinth to the twenty-first-century church worldwide. In 1 Corinthians 12:13, Paul refers to the church as a body consisting of many differing members, likening it to the human body, which consists of a variety of members (i.e., a foot, a hand, an ear, or an eye—see verses 15–16).

When it comes to caring for the body of Christ, a good rule of thumb is to do what's best for the body. Just as the human body is bigger than any one of its parts, so a body of believers is more and bigger than any single member. What's best for an individual member must be considered in the context of what's best for the body at large. Just as physical body parts are varied in shape and size and have specific functions, the members of the body of Christ are different and have specific spiritual gifts for the benefit of the body as a whole. Thus, what's best for the body is what ought to matter to each individual member.

Americans live in a culture of individualism. Our "me, myself, and I" society allows individual desires or needs to trump corporate or group desires or needs. For example, individual family members, be they parents or children, may value themselves more than the family at large; individual believers or church members may see themselves as more important than the church body as a whole. Although God is interested in the desires and needs of his individual children or family members, he is more committed to the body of believers or church family, a representation of the bride of Christ. Like the human body, the church is a body consisting of many members. God's priority is what's best for the body rather than the individual body parts or members. Paul wrote in 1 Corinthians 12:14 and in 12:19–20, "For the body does not consist of one member, but of many ... If all were a single member, where would the body be? As it is, there are many parts, yet one body." These verses emphasize the priority of the body over and above any individual member. The guiding and governing question in pastoral congregational ministry is, "What's best for the body?"

Unfortunately, a secular culture pursuing what's best for the individual has seeped into the church. This is contrary to what Paul wrote in Philippians 2:3–5 to a first-century local church: "Do nothing from selfish ambition or conceit, but in humility count others more significant than yourselves. Let each of you look not only to his own interests, but also to the interests of others. Have this mind among yourselves, which is yours in Christ Jesus." In verse 5, "this mind" refers to the first four verses that describe an attitude, disposition, or posture of humility. At the foundation of a successful pastoral transition is the commitment by the leadership and the congregation to practice one another passages of the New Testament in order to cultivate a culture of Christlike humility. This is what's best for the body.

In my third pastorate, I preached a sermon series entitled "One Another Living in the Church," featuring several one another passages in the New Testament. God had impressed upon me the need for our church family to know and embrace these practical truths for more-effective biblical living and mutually beneficial ministry. What should one-another living in the church look like? How does this play out in the Christian community? What is one-another living like day to day?

While studying one another passages in the New Testament, I discovered a primary relationship recorded in Romans 12:3–5 explaining that we are *members* of one another: "For by the grace given to me I say to everyone among you not to think of himself more highly than he ought to think, but to think with sober judgment, each according to the measure of faith that God has assigned. For as in one body, we have many members, and the members do not all have the same function, so we, though many, are one body in Christ, *and individually members one of another*" (emphasis added).

Then, in John 13:34–35, I discovered a primary responsibility based on that relationship. Christians are to love another as Christ loved us: "A new commandment I give to you, that you love one another: just as I have loved you, you also are to love one another. By this all people will know that you are my disciples, if you have love for one another" (John 13:34–35). The other one-another passages unpack what it means to love others as members of one-another.

The relationship is membership with three key implications found in Romans 12:3–5. First, membership implies plurality. There are "*many* members" (verse 4, emphasis added). The family of God consists of every born-again person since the day of Pentecost. Fifty days after the resurrection of Jesus Christ, the church was born and has been growing ever since. It's a global body with many members. Second, membership implies diversity: "the members do not all have the same function" (Romans 12:4). Every member of God's family is different. No single member of the human body can function effectively apart from the rest of the body, and no individual Christian can function effectively by him- or herself. Furthermore, no one member of Christ's body is more important than any other. Though differences can make life difficult and frustrating, being different is not wrong. God made us different on purpose, and our differences are strengths, not weaknesses. Each of us is a necessary part of the body. Third, membership implies unity— "so we, being many, are one body in Christ … members one of another" (Romans 12:5). The family of God is unified: one for all, and all for one! Christians should work hard at cultivating unity, "eager to maintain the unity of the Spirit in the bond of peace" (Ephesians 4:1–3). Sameness or uniformity should be avoided, but unity is essential. Philipp Melanchthon, a contemporary of and collaborator with Martin Luther in the Protestant Reformation, said, "In essentials, unity; in differences, liberty; in all things, charity." Differences should not divide us but rather unite us. They should not weaken us but strengthen us. Differences are a testimony to the creativity and ingenuity of God.

In his book *31 Ways to be A "One Another" Christian,* Dr. Stuart Scott on page 11 comments, "People, created in the image of God, are made for relationships. Although the term 'relationship' does not appear as a word in most modern translations of the Bible, the concept is found in all the books of the Bible. The term 'one another' is repeated numerous times in the New Testament—and always in a way that demonstrates how one believer is to relate (or be in a certain relationship) to another believer." Christians are not to go it alone but to live in relationship with one another. We live most effectively in community, not in isolation. Individualism may be

"American," but it's neither biblical nor Christian. The church is a called-out assembly of believers, a gathering of saints for the purpose of teaching and learning biblical doctrine, practicing fellowship, observing the ordinances, and offering prayers (Acts 2:42). Just as a human body consists of many members with differing functions, so the church is a body of many members but with only one head, Jesus Christ.

The responsibility to love one another is declared by Jesus in John 13:34–35. Love is a responsible action and a choice we make. It's an act of the will and not primarily a feeling. We are to love one another whether we feel like it or not. Why? Because love is primarily volitional, not emotional. Love purposes to do what's best for another person regardless of the perceived worthiness of a person and his or her response or lack of response. Five times in the gospels and eleven times in the epistles, we are commanded to love one another. That makes it very important and something we are morally obligated to do.

There are three aspects to the responsibility of loving one another according to John 13:34–35. First, love is *commanded*. Jesus said, "A new commandment I give to you." Loving one another is an act of obedience, not a matter of convenience. Although it's good to feel loving toward each other, we are to love one another even when we don't feel like it. Love is never optional. Second, love is *Christlike*. Jesus said, "Just as I have loved you." Jesus modeled this love, and we are to love like him. He's the standard of love (Ephesians 5:25). Our love is to compare to Christ's and not someone else's. Third, love is *characteristic*. "By this all people will know that you are my disciples, if you have love for one another" (John 13:35). Amazingly, Jesus gave the world the right to judge believers according to how they love each other. This marks a believer more than anything else. Others will know we are Christians by our love. In *The Mark of a Christian*, Francis Schaeffer wrote, "Our relationship with each other is the criterion the world uses to judge whether our message is truthful—Christian community is the final apologetic." Loving one another is the best defense for Christianity. One-another living is a relationship and a responsibility. As members of one another, we are to love each another.

The apostle Paul frequently evaluated a church's growth and maturity based on its love life (1 Thessalonians 1:3, 3:12, 4:9–10). When Paul analyzed a church, the bottom line was love (Colossians 3:14, "Above all, put on love"). All the other one-another exhortations demonstrate love in action. They teach us how to love one another by preferring one another, bearing one another's burdens, serving one another, praying for one another, submitting to one to another, and in many other ways. Three observations about one another verses in the New Testament are:

1. Each one represents *a particular responsibility* every believer has toward other members of the body. No one is exempt, and all are accountable to our Father, God. We need each other! We're friends and family.
2. Each one is *a commandment or expectation*, not a suggestion or an option or something nice to do if we feel like it. Choosing not to do these things is disobedience or sin.
3. Each one marks believers as belonging to Christ, and these are *distinguishing characteristics* of a Christian lifestyle. This is true Christlikeness. This is the fleshing out of the fruit of the Spirit (Galatians 5:22–23).

In considering Roman 12:10, "outdo one another in showing honor," we need to understand not only what this means, but how it looks and how we are to live in a one-another family or community relationship. Consequently, there are principles that need to be reinforced in the lives of God's people:

1. Christians are body members that belong to the same body, Christ's body, and are to look and live like it by loving God and loving people. This fulfills the greatest and first

commandment of all: Love God whole-heartedly. It also fulfills the second one: Love your neighbor as yourself (Matthew 22:34–39).

2. Christians are body members that complement each other or fit together having the goal of always doing *what's best for the body*. One-another living is a life of JOY: Jesus, Others, and You. It is "others-minded," which is the disposition, attitude, or mind of Christ (Philippians 2:1–5).

3. Christians are body members that are to function effectively together, contributing to the strength, health, and growth of the body. Serving together is better and it gets more done for Jesus's sake.

It was the second principle that became a primary part of my philosophy of pastoral ministry. Pastors, deacons, and church members are to filter all they do through the question, "What's best for the body?" The "me, myself, and mine" culture in which we live too often shows up in the church in the form of "This is my ministry" or "I'm not getting anything out of the sermons, and I don't like the songs" or "I'd like some recognition for all I do around here." Rather, the local church should be a counterculture to the secular one in which we live. The prevailing attitude should be marked by, "I am here to serve" versus "What can you do for me?" And by, "How can I help you," versus "Why don't more people offer to help me?" And by, "What can I give?" versus "I don't get enough credit or recognition."

It is this principle that drove me in my quest for a better pastoral transition model. It is *not* best for the body to be blindsided by a pastor, following months of clandestine conversations with another church, who then announces on a Sunday morning that he is resigning because he has accepted a call to pastor another congregation. It is *not* best for the body to be thrust into a pastoral search mode and then experience months, if not years, of pastorless ministry. It's *not* best for the body to have a smorgasbord of pulpit supply stretching over months or longer. It may, however, be best for the body to have an interim pastorate where a local church has a steady diet of pulpit ministry from the same man who also can provide consistency of pastoral leadership and congregational care.

What is best for the body is a relatively seamless transition from one person to another following years—or at least months—of mentoring a person to succeed him as pastor. In two of my four pastorates, I had the privilege of mentoring my successors as lead pastors. In the first, the man who followed me was an intern for almost a year before being called as an associate pastor. For a total of six years, he and I served together, and I was able to mentor him. When that church called him as its lead pastor, he was ready, and it was best for that body of believers. He served as lead pastor there for the next eighteen years.

In the second, I was called by the church specifically to mentor and prepare the associate pastor to become the next lead pastor. For seven years, we served together in a mutually beneficial pastoral partnership. He was a submissive and effective associate pastor with the abilities and gifts to be a lead pastor. In a relatively seamless transition (see Appendix B for more details), he was called to be their lead pastor. I became the associate. It was a well-conceived plan, and the process worked. It's what was best for that body of believers.

This part of my ministry philosophy was born out of learning the pastoral ministry ropes somewhat the hard way. I never was an intern or an associate pastor, but I cut my teeth on a struggling local church just three months away from dissolving. I pastored there for seven years before having a summer pastoral intern who then was called as my assistant. I began my next two pastorates as the only pastor on staff, but then added associate pastors and mentored seminary interns.

Over forty years of pastoral experience, I grew in valuing interns and associate pastors. The men I mentored provided valuable assistance to me as the lead pastor and were assets to the respective local churches with their shepherding skills. Each church grew stronger and increased in numbers under capable, competent pastoral leadership. It was my privilege to have an assistant in my first pastorate, one intern and two associates in my second pastorate, and nine interns and two associates in my third pastorate. I concluded my pastoral experience beginning as the lead pastor and ending as one of two associate pastors. Thus, I finished where I always wished I had started, as an associate pastor. But God's will for me was to learn and lead in a different way.

I will always be grateful for those believers who patiently allowed me to grow as a lead pastor. I began as a very "green" pastor and slowly matured in my pastoral role and responsibilities. In my first pastorate, my two-year-old daughter, who was beginning to memorize Psalm 23, asked me one day, "Daddy, are you a green pasture?" I replied, "Yes, honey, as green as they come." And I was. But I ripened or matured over forty-two years, bearing fruit that has remained. To God be the glory for his work of redemption and sanctification in my life, and for giving me the privilege of shepherding his flock in four different locations. The extent to which I have endeavored to pastor in a way that's best for the body is the extent to which I have found fulfillment and been blessed in watching God's people grow and mature in Christ.

2

CHAPTER

A VISION FOR TRANSITION

(Over Forty Years Becoming Clear)

This book has been over forty years in the making. I've learned many things about pastoral ministry in the four local churches I have pastored. Some of those lessons were learned the hard way. But, to personalize an insurance company's slogan, "I know a thing or two because I've seen a thing or two." One thing I know for sure is that the church is God's flock to be pastored or shepherded carefully and lovingly. Jesus is the chief shepherd of His sheep who are to be nurtured by gifted men who are called to be pastor-teachers. I am not indispensable, but I am responsible to do what's best for the body and its spiritual well-being. I am accountable to Jesus as well as to the church because someday I will give an account for how I watched over the souls of the saints I pastored (Hebrews 13:17). Pastors should give oversight willingly and eagerly and lead by example (1 Peter 5:2–3).

David Culver

THE TRANSITION PROCESS

Pastoral leadership changes happen, but they don't always go well. A thoughtful and prayerful transition process contributes to an effective leadership transition. Local churches that follow a carefully crafted process, purposing to do what's best for the body of Christ and not what is purely expedient, are more apt to realize good results. They are set up well for experiencing unity in the community, calling a person well-suited for that congregation and long-term ministry effectiveness.

Here are ten marks of a transition process that sets up a congregation for a positive pastoral change:

- A church with a vision for consistency in pastoral leadership. A local church that will look ahead and anticipate the changes to come will handle change and transition much better.
- A leadership team committed to developing a pastoral staff for mentoring and training the next leaders. This is a commitment to discipleship or the growing and maturing of fully devoted followers of Jesus Christ.
- A pastoral staff with a team spirit committed to providing Christlike pastoral leadership and care. A lead pastor and associate pastors must have a team mentality that sees pastoral ministry as a partnership. In my last three pastorates, I had the joy of experiencing this team spirit that was cultivated through weekly pastors' meetings as well as by enjoying more informal fellowship, such as on the golf course or backyard barbecue.
- A respect for and commitment to following church polity and constitutional procedure, and the valuing of congregational involvement. This can be demonstrated by calling special "family" meetings to share updates and solicit prayer while assuring the people that proper procedure is being followed.

- A commitment to consistent, clear communication between church leadership and the congregation. There are no substitutes for effective communication. In the real estate world, the motto is, "Location, location, location." In the local church community, it is, "Communicate, communicate, communicate." Uninformed people are not happy people. With a lack of communication, church members become confused and frustrated. Never underestimate the importance of communication and do it more often than seems necessary.

- Transparent, trustworthy leadership that cultivates the congregation's confidence and trust. Transparency builds trust, and people will follow leaders with vision and whom they trust. Nothing engenders confidence in leadership more than consistent full disclosure about a search process. A church family trusts pastors and deacons who value its inclusion demonstrated by written and verbal communication.

- Seasoned, experienced, and proven pastoral leadership dedicated to training people for pastoral ministry. This is the Barnabas-Saul and Paul-Timothy approach to leadership training (see chapter 8). Nothing takes the place of experience, and experience shared is priceless.

- Teachable young people who want to learn from those who are experienced in pastoral ministry. A winning combination in a local assembly requires experienced pastors willing to mentor and teachable younger people willing to be mentored.

- Humble people who don't care who gets the credit and are committed to what's best for the body and the testimony of Jesus Christ. Humility literally refers to something that does not rise from the ground. It is a must in leadership as it is like Jesus Christ, who humbled himself from the cradle to the cross.

- A commitment to following biblical principles for local church leadership transitions. Tevia, in *Fiddler on the Roof,* exclaimed, "Tradition!" but then learned that tradition is not always what's best. A traditional approach to pastoral transitions not based on biblical principles is decidedly not what's best for the body.

A MEMORABLE MEETING

I recall the night the Shawnee Hills Baptist Church (SHBC) leadership team, two pastors and nine deacons, met to receive the recommendation of the pastoral search team that had been doing its homework the previous four months. The current associate pastor of SHBC was recommended to be the candidate for senior or lead pastor. The leadership team unanimously approved the search team's recommendation and purposed to present it to the voting membership the following Sunday evening. That night, I shared a prepared statement with the other men. It was from my heart, communicating what to expect from me when the roles reversed and I became an associate pastor. I called it "The Transition," and read it to them:

> Lord willing, within the next four to five months, our associate pastor will be the lead pastor and I will be the associate pastor. Although we believe this to be the will of God, it's going to be different, awkward, and take time to adjust to—for all of us. I have had an associate follow me as the lead pastor, but I've not stayed and become the associate. Furthermore, I've never been an associate pastor and he's never had the permanent responsibility of being a lead pastor. Also, you haven't experienced this kind of transition before and neither has the

church family. Thus, I've tried to think of what we need to anticipate as a leadership team when the transition takes place. I'd like to share four things in anticipation of a transition.

1. **The buck will stop with the new lead pastor.** He will assume the primary leadership of the church and I will defer to him. He will be the one to lead monthly leadership team meetings and weekly staff meetings. He will meet with the chairman of the leadership team (LT) to set the agenda for monthly LT meetings. He will be the one to set the direction for this local church with our input and counsel and will assume the pastoral leadership of the administrative team.

2. **I will assist the new lead pastor in the pastoral leadership and care of this church family.** My role will be to take direction from him and carry out the responsibilities of my associate's role accordingly. He and I have already begun talking about this, and I have assured him that I will follow his lead and encourage others to do the same. I will be a "bench coach" as needed, but he will be the "head coach." If, for whatever reason, my role is a distraction or hindrance to his leadership and ministry, I will retire before the projected time.

3. **The new lead pastor will be the primary preacher, and I will preach as requested and/ or assigned by him.** Admittedly, this will not be easy as I love to preach and look forward to it every time. But I have no reservations about following his lead in this way. He will choose the texts and set the preaching schedule and

calendar. I will be at his service just as he has
been at mine the past seven years.

4. **The new lead pastor will cast the vision
God has given him for this church, and I
will support him in trusting God to fulfill
that vision.** I expect he will implement new
initiatives and directives of his own. I trust him
and am confident he will cast a vision that is
biblically sound and consistent with what is best
for the body for the glory of God.

Each of us on this leadership team needs to
lead by example, demonstrating Proverbs 3:5–6
confidence in the Lord and respect for the pastor's
leadership. This Sunday night's state-of-the-church
meeting is an opportunity to model being "eager
to maintain the unity of the spirit in the bond of
peace" (Ephesians 4:3). We must stand shoulder-to-
shoulder and arm-in-arm in our presentation of our
associate pastor as *the* candidate for senior or lead
pastor. We must be men of prayer, lifting up holy
hands without anger or quarreling. We must be
men of faith as we look unto Jesus, the author and
finisher of our faith, that the people of Shawnee
Hills Baptist Church can trust to lead them through
this transition and then forward. I do believe the
best is yet come for our local church.

That being shared, many of their concerns were allayed. This
only confirmed the importance and value of both being transparent
and providing the information they needed to continue processing
the transition and anticipating what pastoral leadership would look
like when our roles were exchanged.

Vision is an interesting thing. I am not referring to physical vision, eyesight, or clairvoyance, but to spiritual or mental vision that is an idea or picture of the future or what one hopes is going to happen. A clear vision helps us in pursuing dreams and achieving goals. I have worked with contractors in house remodeling projects who could "see" how our kitchen or screened-in porch would look before construction began. I have also served with people in ministry who, with the eyes of faith, "see" what God can do and what they believe he will do. A friend of mine with the gift of faith has said of someone who is close to believing in Jesus for eternal life, "He is going to get saved; he just doesn't know it yet." That's vision based on faith.

Before coming into focus, a vision is blurry, lacking clarity and definition. With time and experience, a vision sharpens and gains specificity. Forty years ago, my vision of pastoral transitions was quite black and white, a bit blurry, and very limited in its scope. Over the years, color was added, and it became clearer and more defined. I'm not sure a vision is ever fully developed or defined, but mine is much sharper and more colorful. I thank God for giving me both ears to hear his truth and eyes to see his vision of a pastoral leadership transition. Local churches that will embrace it will find it is what's best for the body.

PLANNING YOURSELF OUT OF A JOB
(A Purposeful Process)

There is a basic attitude adjustment that needs to take place for a pastoral transition to be successful. It is this: a pastor must know that he is not indispensable but is replaceable; that he is not essential but integral to the health and growth of a local church; and that he is not the end-all but a means to an end of equipping the saints for the work of ministry (Ephesians 4:12–16). Sooner or later, every pastor is replaced, either because of changing ministries, health limitations, or retirement. This indicates that he is not essential but is very useful in preparing the body of believers for the next lead pastor or shepherd. The local church neither rises nor sets on the pastor. Rather, he is a means (or a minister) that God is using for the purpose of feeding and leading his sheep. A humble-hearted pastor who recognizes his own limitations is one whom God uses to prepare others to follow Jesus, the chief shepherd, with effectiveness. The pastor who fails to prepare himself and church family for his successor is not wise and may see himself as indispensable.

In other words, a pastor needs to be planning himself out of a job from the time he begins a ministry. Praying and planning for a replacement or successor is what's best for the body. This keeps a person from feeling threatened or selfishly clinging to a position that ultimately hinders the growth and health of a local church. Many pastors have stayed too long, losing confidence in their own abilities as well as the respect of the congregation. This is not to imply that longevity in pastoral ministry cannot be good. Pastoral ministries spanning decades have proven to be what's best for that body of believers. But I am suggesting that refusing to prepare and plan without anticipating change and transition is not what's best for the body. Such lack of foresight sets up a church to plateau, at best, or to decline or die, at worst.

Since my second pastoral ministry, I have endeavored to position a church to be healthy in order to grow spiritually and numerically. Here are several things I personally tried to put into place in anticipation of my departure:

- **Know my strengths and weaknesses** and those of the church body, envisioning the kind of leadership that would lovingly shepherd the church to the next level.
- **Cultivate a humble spirit** by never forgetting that the church I pastor is "the flock of God" (1 Peter 5:2), not mine, and that I am accountable first to Christ, "the chief shepherd" (1 Peter 5:4), and then to the body of believers I am shepherding (Hebrews 13:17).
- **Surround myself with those who are more competent than I**, in some ways—especially those of local church leadership and pastoral staff members. A pastor must not be threatened by another's competency. Rather, he should be thankful for God's provision of skillful shepherds.
- **Purpose not to stay beyond my effectiveness** and know when it's time to transition or leave. My wife is the one I count on the most, as she knows me the best. But I must be honest with myself in knowing when I'm no longer functioning effectively or providing the kind of pastoral care and leadership that is best for the body. As I approached

retirement, I knew I was losing patience, energy, and stamina for pastoral ministry. I purposed to finish strong and well. I prayed to know when to step aside, and God made that very clear. I desired that and didn't dread it.

- **Clearly communicate a plan** to the church leadership to give them time to adjust to the idea and ask questions. In my last pastorate, I served the church leadership a five-year notice of my planned retirement. During many leadership and congregational meetings, I referenced the plan for transition before my retirement. I tried to mention it often.

Too often, a pastoral change comes unexpectedly or without advance notice. The church leadership is not in the know, let alone the church family. A decision is made by the pastor, either to leave for another church, or to retire or to resign with nowhere to go. This leaves the church in a lurch. With no forewarning, the church body is left to scramble to fill the void as soon as possible. Often, the congregation moves too quickly, settling for a person who is not a good fit and who becomes a sacrificial lamb in preparation for the one to follow.

I saw this happen in one of my former pastorates. Although that local assembly had the foresight to call a seasoned man as an interim, they made several serious mistakes. First, they changed the church's constitution on Bible version preference. Caution that was given against making any constitutional changes prior to calling the next pastor was disregarded. Secondly, the search committee pursued a man who was available to pastor but who was not the best fit for that church. Out of convenience and expedience, the church asked that man to fill the pulpit and subsequently asked him to candidate. This all happened quickly. The man was personable and humorous and was called as the next pastor. But, three years later, the church found itself in another pastoral search. From then on, the church declined and eventually settled for a string of part-time pastors as the congregation dwindled to a handful of people. Good, solid, and faithful members left for other local churches, and the foundation crumbled.

Years ago, I accepted an invitation to speak at the thirtieth anniversary of this local church. The pastor was a full-time custodian at a local public school and was part-time at the church. At the celebration, many former members attended who had previously left because of a traditional style of pastoral leadership that majored on the minors. Unfortunately, although the church still exists, the current pastor is part-time, as the congregation is too small to provide full-time support. It is a sad tale of a church without a plan for a good pastoral transition that could not recover and that continues to struggle with only a handful in attendance.

Purposeful pastoral transitions that are prayerfully planned have a much higher success rate. Such transitions are providential, not accidental. They are intentional, not spontaneous. They are neither random nor haphazard. God is not a God of confusion but of peace, and he desires that all things within the church be done decently and in order (1 Corinthians 14:33, 40). Too often, church transitions are reactionary and confusing, lacking peace and harmony. For lack of a prayerfully and purposefully wrought transition plan, a church will find that things are not done decently and in order. In the following chapters, a more decent and orderly succession and transition plan is described that minimizes confusion and maximizes unity and peace in the body.

4

CHAPTER

THE PROCESS IS THE GOAL

(We See a Process; God Sees the Goal)

The familiar adage "Don't miss the forest for the trees" is also true in reverse: "Don't miss the trees for the forest." A forest consists of many trees, usually of different species, heights, and widths. If we're not careful, all we'll see is the forest and fail to appreciate the variety of trees that make up the forest. After my oldest daughter got her first pair of eyeglasses as a child, she walked outside and exclaimed, "Wow! I see trees!" Before she got eyeglasses, all the trees ran together, making one big, long tree. Now she could see each one. My wife and I literally cried, as we hadn't realized what she was missing because of her poor eyesight. But we also rejoiced because now she could see more clearly. In her case, the process of an eye examination, the prescription for new glasses, and the purchasing of eyeglasses was the goal. Seeing trees was a wonderful outcome, but it was not the goal.

The goal of a pastoral transition is a purposeful process, not simply finding another pastor as soon as possible. Too many congregations sacrifice the permanent on the altar of the expedient. When a search committee's goal is to narrow multiple resumes down to one to have a candidate sooner than later, their goal differs from

God's. The product or outcome (i.e., getting a pastor) is too often seen as the goal. It is not. The process is the goal, for without the right process, you'll have the wrong outcome or pastor. More than a few local churches have settled for an unsuitable pastor in preference for following a "fast-lane" process. Furthermore, an expedited pastoral search may overlook someone within the church family who is what's best for the body but who needs time to develop and mature.

God's purpose is more about the process than the product. Preparation is what makes culmination possible. I first realized this when reading the July 28 entry of *My Utmost for His Highest* by Oswald Chambers. Here's what he wrote (emphasis is mine):

> We tend to think that if Jesus Christ compels us to do something and we are obedient to Him, He will lead us to great success. We should never have the thought that our dreams of success are God's purpose for us. In fact, His purpose may be exactly the opposite. We have the idea that God is leading us toward a particular end or a desired goal, but He is not. The question of whether or not we arrive at a particular goal is of little importance, and reaching it becomes merely an episode along the way. What we see as only the process of reaching a particular end, God sees as the goal itself.
>
> What is my vision of God's purpose for me? Whatever it may be, His purpose is for me to depend on Him and on His power *now*. If I can stay calm, faithful, and unconfused while in the middle of the turmoil of life, the goal of the purpose of God is being accomplished in me. God is not working toward a particular finish—His purpose is the process itself. What He desires for me is that I see "Him walking on the sea" with no shore, no success, nor goal in sight, but simply having the absolute

certainty that everything is all right because I see "Him walking on the sea" (Mark 6:49). It is the process, not the outcome, that is glorifying to God.

God's training is for now, not later. His purpose is for this very minute, not for some time in the future. We have nothing to do with what will follow our obedience, and we are wrong to concern ourselves with it. What people call preparation, God sees as the goal itself.

God's purpose is to enable me to see that He can walk on the storms of my life right now. If we have a further goal in mind, we are not paying enough attention to the present time. However, if we realize that moment-by-moment obedience is the goal, then each moment as it comes is precious.

When it comes to a pastoral change or transition, too often, the actual change or new ministry is seen as the goal. Instead, that is the outcome, not the goal. The process is the goal since it will determine the actual outcome and whether the desired outcome happens. But frequently, the pastor's goal is to change churches as soon as possible, without regard for how this will affect the congregation he is leaving or how to best prepare that church for its next pastor. Getting to Church B from Church A as soon as possible is seen as the goal, when, in fact, the means itself is what matters most. The determined means will make all the difference in the outcome and whether what's best for the body happens and not just what's best for the individual.

In planning a pastoral transition, the following things need to be considered on behalf of the church experiencing the change of a pastor and/or the loss of a shepherd.

- Given the church's current culture and health, what's the next level to which that church should aspire? Does it need to be more evangelistic and concentrate on outreach, or does it need to focus on discipleship? Does it need to improve its worship music or develop its children's ministries? Does it need better congregational care versus an effective visitation program? These are just some examples of what might need to be considered before the search for a new pastor begins.

- How is the church doing financially? Can it support a pastor and his family full-time, or should it consider an interim pastor or a missionary pastor who does not need full support for the church to get on better financial footing?

- This begs the question, "Is an interim pastor a better next step?" The goal should never be, "Let's get another pastor ASAP." The liabilities of that are huge, as a church may simply settle for someone who is available but may not be what they need long-term. The assets or benefits of an interim pastor are many, such as:

  o An interim provides immediate, short-term pastoral leadership giving consistency in pulpit ministry and needed guidance overall.

  o An interim gives the church time to determine what kind of pastor it needs and to organize a search.

  o An interim's short-term but intentional ministry assures the church that nothing will be done hastily or prematurely and without opportunity for congregational input.

  o An interim's patient presence and steady leadership takes the pressure off finding a person sooner than later, giving space for needed evaluation.

If there is a liability to having an interim, it is that the people may get comfortable with the interim and become lax in their search. An interim must make it clear from the beginning that he is not an alternative to a long-term pastor and should, from the outset, establish a basic timeline for how long he intends to stay.

Open-ended interim ministries fail to keep appropriate pressure on the local church to find a pastor within a reasonable timeframe.

In Charles Spurgeon's classic devotional, *Morning* and *Evening*, the May 24 entry is based on Psalm 138:8, "The Lord will fulfill his purpose for me." Spurgeon wrote:

> The confidence that the psalmist expresses is a *divine confidence*. He did not say, "I have enough grace to perfect that which concerns me—my faith is so steady that it will not falter—my love is so warm that it will never grow cold—my resolution is so firm that nothing can move it." No, his dependence was on the Lord alone. If we display a confidence that is not grounded on the Rock of ages, our confidence is worse than a dream; it will fall upon us and cover us with its ruins, to our sorrow and confusion.
>
> The psalmist was wise; he rested on nothing less than the *Lord's* work. It is the Lord who has begun the good work within us; it is He who has carried it on; and if He does not finish it, it never will be completed. If there is one stitch in the celestial garment of our righteousness that we must insert ourselves, then we are lost; but this is our confidence—what the Lord begins, He completes. He *has* done it all, *must* do it all, and *will* do it all. Our confidence must not be in what we have done, nor in what we have resolved to do, but entirely in what *the Lord* will do.
>
> Unbelief insinuates: "You will never be able to stand. Look at the evil of your heart—you can never conquer sin; remember the sinful pleasures and temptations of the world that beset you—you will be certainly allured by them and led astray."

> True, we would certainly perish if left to our own
> strength. If by ourselves we navigate the frailest
> vessels of our lives over so rough a sea, we might
> well give up the voyage in despair; but thanks be to
> God, He will complete that which concerns us and
> bring us to the desired haven. We can never be too
> confident when we confide in Him alone, and never
> too eager to have such a trust.

Spurgeon references a "divine confidence" that rests in God's work, his plan, and purpose for us—not our own. What God begins, God finishes. With that in mind, when a local church plans and purposes to mentor people for ministry, the leadership and congregation must have a divine confidence that sees the process as the goal. Even if the outcome is different than what was expected, the goal was realized in the process that was followed.

Again, in the July 28 *My Utmost for His Highest* devotional, Chambers writes, "God's training is for now, not later. His purpose is for this very minute, not for some time in the future. We have nothing to do with what will follow our obedience, and we are wrong to concern ourselves with it. What people call preparation God sees as the goal itself." We must be careful not to look past or beyond the process prematurely to the final product or outcome, and thus miss what God has to teach us presently. While God has a will to perform and a desired outcome, his goal is that we learn and grow through the process itself. That's what's best for the body.

5

CHAPTER

NOT SEAMLESS, BUT CLOSE

(Insider or Outsider?)

Note: I have chosen to refer to the men in this chapter by their first names only.

Sometimes the obvious is overlooked or seemingly invisible during a search. My wife is mystified over how many times I fail to see what's right in front of me. I will search in vain for a can of crushed pineapple in the pantry, only for her to find it within seconds. Or for her to ask me to pick up a box of tapioca at the grocery store and tell me which aisle and section, only for me to call her because I can't find it and am convinced the store doesn't carry it. Reluctantly, I agree to ask a female store employee, who goes directly to it and hands it to me, smiling, and says, "My husband would not have seen it either." (By the way, even though tapioca is with the Jell-o and puddings, it's not easy to find.)

This occurs in local churches where a senior pastor is leaving or retiring. A pastoral search team is commissioned to find a candidate from the outside even though there may be experienced and qualified associates on staff who may be overlooked in the search. Too often, an internal candidate is never considered because he doesn't fit the model of a traditional pastoral search process. Where there are two or more pastors on staff, the search should begin at close range, giving at least preliminary consideration to a pastor who has proven shepherding skills. Unfortunately, some churches intentionally ignore the other pastor(s) on staff, wanting a clean slate or at least to minimize the qualifications and skills of an associate.

Jon was a seminary student the first time I met him, and he became my first intern. He served for nine months with me before being called as an associate pastor with me. I remember telling the director of internships at the seminary that Jon attended, "I want a keeper." The director assured me he would give me his best, and he did. Jon and I served together for the next six years before the Lord called me to a local assembly in another state as its lead pastor. But I had mentored Jon to succeed me as lead pastor long before I sensed God preparing my wife and me to make a ministry move. Providentially, God led that congregation to call Jon as its next lead pastor. He was an "inside man" who proved to be God's man to serve there another eighteen years.

At the next church, Jason was a member and a seminary student working with the teens. We customized a two-year internship for him to serve in student ministries. At the end of those two years, he received a unanimous call to become the pastor of student ministries, where he served the next ten years. Again, he was an "inside man" who proved to be God's man to serve on the pastoral staff along with me and the other associate pastor.

From the beginning of my final pastoral ministry, I mentored Adam to be the next lead pastor. He had been a member of that local church since he was a college student and before he was married. After getting married, he served as a deacon and then as a youth leader before being called as a part-time youth pastor. In February 2012, the church called him to serve full time as the youth pastor. Two weeks later, the senior pastor resigned, and he became the pastor, filling the gap until I was called a year later. Even though he was considered for the next lead pastor, the church opted for me to come and mentor him to follow me. By the grace of God, that is what happened. Seven years later, the church called him to be the lead pastor, and I transitioned to associate. He was an "inside man" prepared by God over the previous fifteen years.

On the night our associate pastor was announced to the congregation as the candidate for senior pastor, I closed the meeting with the following statement:

> Seven years ago, at the age of sixty-one, I was asked to candidate for the position of senior pastor. In the providence of God and for such a time as this God called Carolyn and me to this church family.
>
> Seven years ago, the church family was fragmented due to a critical time of pastoral leadership transition that left this congregation without a pastor. Carolyn and I were fragmented, too, because of a ministry crisis of our own, leaving us wondering what, if any, ministry might be in our future. One month shy of seven years ago, we were called to come here. An understood expectation was that I would mentor Pastor Adam to be the next senior pastor. A time frame was not determined then, yet it was the hope of the leadership team that within five to ten years that transition might happen.
>
> Well, it's close. In less than two months, our associate pastor will candidate as the next senior pastor. It has been my privilege and joy to mentor him, though I have learned and grown by his example and ministry partnership. I do not know how a pastoral team relationship could have been any better or more mutually beneficial than ours. It's been a father-son relationship and a pastoral-peer relationship marked by mutual love and respect. If it is the Lord's will for him to succeed me as senior

pastor, I can assure you that, by the grace of God, our relationship as beloved brothers in Christ will not change. Our ministry roles may change, but our common commitment to co-shepherd God's flock, Shawnee Hills, will not waver.

In closing, I will borrow Paul's word to the assembly of believers in Thessalonica recorded in 2 Thessalonians 3:1–5 as the testimony of our associate pastor and me, "Finally, brothers and sisters, pray for us, that the word of the Lord may speed ahead and be honored ... the Lord is faithful. He will establish and guard you against the evil one. And we have confidence in the Lord about you ... May the Lord direct your hearts to the love of God and to the steadfastness of Christ. Amen."

In each of the three scenarios, Jon, Jason, and Adam were "inside men" rather than unknowns brought in from the outside. They were loved and respected by their respective church families and became pastors proving to be what was best for the body. Although this is not possible in every local church, it may be more probable if there is a vision for training up and mentoring "inside men" for pastoral ministry. There is biblical precedent for this as it relates to Joshua being mentored by Moses to lead Israel, or Timothy who was mentored by Paul to pastor the church in Ephesus. In each case, a known insider, rather than an unknown outsider, proved to be the right person at the right time. Paul's words to Timothy in 1 Timothy 2:2 say it best, "And what you have heard from me in the presence of many witnesses entrust to faithful men, who will be able to teach others also."

Perhaps there's someone right under your nose, an "inside man," whom God is training to become the next pastor of your church. He may be a deacon, youth leader, or Sunday school teacher. Many years ago, a church in central Ohio began a search for a senior pastor. A deacon in that congregation who was a businessperson in the community, became the chairperson of the pastoral search committee. In the course of time, this man's giftedness made it apparent to the search team that he should be considered as a potential candidate for senior pastor. Ultimately, he did candidate, and there was an affirmative vote. He was an "inside man" whom God was preparing to lead and feed that local church family. He went on to serve many years as the church's senior pastor with effective influence on that congregation as well as on churches within the state and national associations.

Watch and pray!

6
CHAPTER

DECREASING ... INCREASING
(The John 3:30 Principle)

When my transition from lead to associate pastor occurred, several well-meaning people asked, "So, how does it feel to be demoted?" That gave me pause, as I had not thought of my new role as a demotion, but it also made me realize that I had been decreased. That was a humbling realization, but it reminded me of what John the baptizer said of himself and Jesus Christ in anticipation of their transition, "He must increase, but I must decrease" (John 3:30). Prior to that, John asserted, "Therefore, this joy of mine is now complete" (John 3:29). John's calling and purpose were to herald the coming of the Messiah and to prepare the way for him. For several years, John was the frontline prophet of God. But now, he was ready to step back to allow Jesus to step forward. The prophet was being eclipsed by the Messiah. John was decreasing, and Jesus was increasing. This was God's will and plan. John was the forerunner of the promised Messiah of Israel who, when he arrived, caused John's role and responsibilities to decrease in terms of notoriety and influence. It was God's plan and the best one.

A transition in pastoral leadership is one of decreasing and increasing. In my case, I was not demoted, but my pastoral role decreased while Adam's increased. This is not to be misconstrued as implying inferiority and superiority. Rather, it is a planned, intentional change of roles and responsibilities to provide what's best for the body. Another example of this decrease-increase principle is seen in the relationship of Barnabas and Saul-turned-Paul. Barnabas, "the son of encouragement," is the one who discipled and mentored the apostle Paul. Barnabas was the forerunner of Paul. Let's meet Barnabas and learn how he and Paul illustrate the John 3:30 decrease-increase transition principle.

A hero is a person who is admired or idealized for courage, outstanding achievements, or noble qualities. One of my heroes is Barnabas (or Joseph), who was a Levite from the island of Cyprus. The apostles nicknamed him Barnabas, "son of encouragement," presumably because of his here-to-help heart (Acts 4:36–37). The word *encouragement* means "to call alongside." The Holy Spirit is the comforter or helper—the same word. Barnabas was a comforter or helper. Got a problem? Call Barnabas. Need help? Ask Barnabas. Need advice and godly counsel? Talk to Barnabas. Granted, you and I may need encouragement ourselves, but we need to be encouragers, too. What or who does that look like? It looks like Barnabas. How?

He encouraged by helping in time of need (Acts 9:23–27). After Saul was saved, his former friends turned on him, plotting to kill him (verses 23–25). And because he had been a persecutor of Christians, the disciples feared him (verse 26). "But Barnabas …" (verse 27a) came alongside Saul, saying, "You're coming with me." This was a critical time in Saul's life, as he was rejected by his former friends and held at arm's length by the disciples. Barnabas stood by Saul, defending him before the apostles (verse 27b). The result of Barnabas' encouragement and defense of Saul was bold preaching and the church being built up (verses 28–31).

He encouraged by investing in the spiritual well-being of other believers (Acts 11:22–23). The Jerusalem church sent Barnabas to Antioch to see what was going on (verses 19–22). There he saw the grace of God, was glad, and encouraged them all to remain faithful to the Lord with steadfast purpose (verse 23). Barnabas was a godly man; that is, God was on his mind, and he was available to be used of the Lord as needed. This inspired description of Barnabas starts on the surface of his life and works inward (verse 24a). He was a good man; that is, he was charitable. He was full of the Holy Spirit or was Spirit-filled and was controlled by the Spirit. He was full of faith (or a man of faith). Then what happened? A great many people were saved (verse 24b). Wow, what fruit! He then went to Tarsus to get Saul to help disciple the new believers, staying for a year teaching many. Interestingly, believers were called Christians first there.

He encouraged by bringing out the best in others (Acts 13–14). Barnabas and Saul were sent out by the Antioch church. It was during this first missionary journey that Saul became Paul and blossomed spiritually (13:1–3). In Acts 9, 11, and 13, it was Barnabas and Saul, in that order. In Acts 13:13ff, it became Paul and Barnabas. There was no apparent jealousy by Barnabas who discipled the apostle Paul. True encouragers make others look better than themselves. An encourager desires to see others using their gifts to glorify God, even if it means being eclipsed in his or her own ministry. Saul eclipsed Barnabas in their work together, but Barnabas didn't object. His focus was not on making a name for himself but rather on seeing God glorified and his work furthered through young men like Saul using their gifts (John 3:30).

He encouraged by loving at all times (Acts 15:36–41). Paul and Barnabas separated over John Mark because Barnabas wanted to give John Mark a second chance and Paul did not. Do believers have conflict with each other? Yes. Were Paul and John Mark ever reconciled? Yes (Colossians 4:10; 2 Timothy 4:11). It would seem that Paul and John Mark became friends through the encouragement of Barnabas. A true friend is honest and speaks the truth in love (Proverbs 17:17).

Barnabas fits the definition of a hero. He is to be admired for his courage as he stood alone in supporting Saul and then stood against Paul in supporting John Mark. He discipled Paul and the believers in Antioch. Also, he is to be commended for his outstanding achievements and noble qualities. He was a Spirit-filled man of faith.

Was I demoted when I became the associate pastor following forty years as a senior or lead pastor? Was I marginalized and considered no longer valuable or essential as a pastor? No more so than were John the Baptist or Barnabas. The increase of one necessitates the decrease of another. But decreasing is not to be equated with becoming invaluable or nonessential. Decreasing, however, does imply humility and a commitment to doing what's best for the body. It's another way of saying what Paul wrote in Philippians 2:1–5: "So, if there is any encouragement in Christ, any comfort from love, any participation in the Spirit, any affection and sympathy, complete my joy by being of the same mind having the same love, being in full accord and of one mind. Do nothing from selfish ambition or conceit, but in humility count others more significant than yourselves. Let each of you look not only to his own interests, but also to the interests of others. Have this mind among yourselves, which is yours in Christ Jesus."

When God the Father planned salvation for his image bearers who had sinned against him and could not reconcile themselves to God, the Father chose an "insider," his Son, the second person of the Holy Trinity to be "the way" (John 14:56). Local churches would do well to look within when anticipating a pastoral change. A person known by a local church and who knows the church may prove to be the right person to be the next lead pastor.

7

CHAPTER

NEW LEADER, SAME LORD

(Some Things Never Change … Thankfully!)

I n Deuteronomy 34:5–6, the death of Moses is recorded. "So Moses, the servant of the LORD, died … and he (the LORD) buried him (Moses)." At the base of Charles Wesley's memorial stone in Westminster Abbey are these words credited to his brother, John: "God buries His workmen; But carries on His work." If anything ought to curb a person's sense of significance or indispensability, it's knowing that he or she is temporary and dispensable. Sooner or later, leaders are replaced because of death, retirement, or disability. Examples of leadership succession are shown throughout the Bible, such as:

- Joshua succeeded Moses as the leader of Israel (see Appendix B).
- Elisha succeeded Elijah as the prophet of God.
- Solomon succeeded David as the king of Israel.
- Paul succeeded Barnabas as the witness to the Gentiles.
- Jesus succeeded John the Baptist as the voice and witness of God.

In each case of transition, there was a change in leadership and a new leader surfaced, but the same Lord continued. Only God is indispensable and irreplaceable. He alone is King of kings and Lord of lords. He is the ultimate and absolute authority, accountable to no one. Isaiah wrote of the coming Messiah, Jesus Christ, that "His name shall be called Wonderful Counselor, Almighty God, Everlasting Father, and Prince of peace. The government shall be upon his shoulder, the increase of which there will be no end" (Isaiah 9:6–7). His throne will never be usurped, and he will never be deposed. Though kings and kingdoms rise and fall, and pastors and churches come and go, the leader of leaders, Jesus Christ, is the same yesterday, today, and forever (Hebrews 13:8).

This truth is comforting and encouraging, reminding us that although some pastors are greatly beloved and highly respected, none is indispensable, and each must someday step aside for another to take his place. The overarching truth that causes followers not to lose heart is that it is the same Lord influencing and leading the new leader. Only God is from everlasting to everlasting (Psalm 90:1–2).

I would like to focus on one of the leadership transitions in the Old Testament that is sometimes overlooked: David to Solomon. David followed Saul and reigned over Israel for forty years, seven years in Hebron, and thirty-three years in Jerusalem. The transition from David to Solomon was vastly different than from Saul to David. David succeeded Saul as Israel's second king because Saul died in battle, although he committed suicide by falling on his own sword. Years before David became king, Samuel anointed him as the next king. But subsequently, David became the singer in Saul's court as well as target practice for Saul in his fits of rage. David was also chased throughout the hills of Judea, hiding in caves while being pursued by Saul.

Before David died, Solomon, the son of Bathsheba, was heir apparent to the throne. The transition from David to Solomon is recorded in 1 Kings 1–3, a transition that was not without conflict and competition. Adonijah, the son of Haggish and brother of

Solomon, exalted himself as king in defiance of David choosing Solomon. Through a series of events involving the prophet Nathan and Bathsheba, as well as David and Nathan, Adonijah's bid for the throne was squelched. Eventually, Adonijah was killed by Solomon's order at the hand of Benaiah.

This is a good reminder that even when there is a clear successor to leadership, whether as king or pastor, there will still be opposition. In the transition from me to our associate becoming lead pastor, neither of us received a unanimous vote. Although both votes were convincing, the results evidenced some opposition or at least hesitancy. Still, the transition took place in a relatively seamless fashion. In a transition like ours, I would expect there to be some push back by those who have never seen this kind of transition or who are not convinced it will work, especially when the former lead pastor stays, as I did.

Back to Solomon. To his credit, Solomon did not aspire to the throne of his father and readily confessed his inadequacy and dependency on the Lord. His words recorded in 1 Kings 3:6–9 are very telling in a good way:

> And Solomon said, "You have shown great and steadfast love to your servant David my father, because he walked before you in faithfulness, in righteousness, and in uprightness of heart toward you. And you have kept for him this great and steadfast love and have given him a son to sit on his throne this day. And now, O Lord my God, you have made your servant king in place of David my father, although I am but a little child. I do not know how to go out or come in. And your servant is in the midst of your people whom you have chosen, a great people, too many to be numbered or counted for multitude. Give your servant therefore an understanding mind to govern your people, that

I may discern between good and evil, for who is able
to govern this your great people?"

Solomon had a humble heart, and he loved God's people. He
wanted what was best for the body, not for himself. Consequently,
God responded by blessing Solomon. God gave him what he asked
for, a wise and discerning mind, as well as what he did not ask for,
riches and honor. The record of this is in 1 Kings 3:10–14:

> It pleased the Lord that Solomon had asked this.
> And God said to him, "Because you have asked
> this, and have not asked for yourself long life or
> riches or the life of your enemies, but have asked
> for yourself understanding to discern what is right,
> behold, I now do according to your word. Behold,
> I give you a wise and discerning mind, so that none
> like you has been before you and none like you shall
> arise after you. I give you also what you have not
> asked, both riches and honor, so that no other king
> shall compare with you, all your days. And if you
> will walk in my ways, keeping my statutes and my
> commandments, as your father David walked, then
> I will lengthen your days."

The principle here is that when we sincerely ask the Lord for what
we need, he blesses, often giving "more abundantly than all that we
ask or think" (Ephesians 3:20). We should never presume upon the
grace of God, but we should always acknowledge the generosity of
our heavenly Father who gives good gifts to his children.

The leadership transition described in this book is a model for
us, showing how God honors a process that is bent on honoring
him and blessing his people. As with Solomon, the goal was not his
becoming king by whatever means. The goal was following a process
that pleased the Lord. So it should be with a pastoral transition.

Pleasing God with a plan and a process that is purposeful and not an end-justifies-the-means effort is also best for the body. The transition process advocated in this book requires humility, putting pride aside and the priority of God's will over ours being done. Things did not unfold just like it had been thought, but what did unfold, resulting in the desired outcome, was better than could have been planned. God's ways are not our ways. They are so much higher and better.

God is sovereign, and Jesus is the head and Lord of his church that he is building. Jesus is the foundation and chief cornerstone, and believers are "living stones," or the building materials used in the construction of building God's church. Ultimately, God will do as he pleases in any given local church, including effecting pastoral transitions and changes. I served in four local churches for more than forty years. God always made it clear when it was time for me to leave and where to go. Though leadership changes happen with pastors resigning, retiring, or going elsewhere, as new leaders are raised up, God does not change. His Lordship is constant. He is from everlasting to everlasting. He is "the blessed and only Sovereign, the King of kings and Lord of lords, who alone has immortality" (1 Timothy 6:15–16).

Pastors come and go, but Jesus Christ is the same, yesterday, today, and forever! That is what's best for the body.

8

CHAPTER

MENTORING INTERNS AND ASSOCIATES
(The Paul-Timothy Model)

Pastoral interns and associate pastors are rich resources for a local church and should be regarded as potential successors rather than just "second men" who may never arrive as lead pastors. Granted, some people because of their giftedness, abilities, education, and goals, never aspire to become senior pastors and are better fitted for a supporting role. But many could transition into being lead pastors if given the opportunity to be trained by others who are seasoned in pastoral ministry and trusted with responsibilities attendant to a lead pastorate. The same principle that applies to medical interns being trained to become doctors or student teachers gaining experience in the classroom to become vocational teachers applies to people being tutored, trained, and mentored to become lead pastors. There's no substitute for experience, and there's no better investment than a lead pastor reproducing himself in another person who may succeed him and surpass him in ministry effectiveness. In writing to the Philippians about Timothy, Paul wrote, "For I have no one like him, who will be genuinely concerned for your welfare…but you know Timothy's proven worth, how as a son with a father he has served with me in the gospel" (Philippians

2:20, 22). Paul mentored Timothy for ministry, reproducing himself in his protégé and then partner in ministry. What a good example of mentoring others for ministry.

How *not* to train an intern or associate can be illustrated by what I call the Saul-David model. In this one, lead pastor "Saul" keeps intern "David" in his place, lest he rise above or replace him. Saul and David's relationship was a strange one at best and a threatening one at worst. On Saul's side, it was a love-hate relationship since, at times, Saul loved having David in his court, playing songs to soothe his spirit. At other times, however, Saul used David for javelin practice or hunted him like an animal of prey throughout the hills of Judea. On David's side, however, it was a relationship of respect for Saul as God's anointed. David had many opportunities to disrespect Saul and even kill him, but he never did. Saul was jealous of David, often treating him with contempt and without justification. Thus, it illustrates the kind of mentor-mentee pairing that is destined for disaster and holds little hope for success.

The Saul-David mentoring model is unenviable, as it is marked by the lead pastor lording it over the intern or associate, treating him as an underling. Intimidation is used as a means of keeping the person in training under the thumb of the senior pastor who is bent on suppressing, not encouraging. This model is designed to maintain control of the intern instead of providing practical and valuable ministry experiences. The interns or associates are given menial tasks or are treated more like custodians or errand runners. This is not what's best for the body. Such "training" is not training at all, but rather a means of ensuring that an intern or an associate never rises above the senior pastor. Sadly, some lead pastors are territorial and are threatened by up-and-coming young people in the ministry who are gifted and are called by God to shepherd his flock. Such lead pastors are often insecure, fearing that a younger minister may win the hearts of "his" people.

A better and more biblical example is the Paul-Timothy model, where there is an iron-sharpening-iron relationship. Paul and

Timothy were like a father and a son who had a mutual love-and-respect relationship. Paul mentored Timothy in word and deed, and Timothy matured spiritually and in ministry under Paul's fatherly counsel and leadership. In this scenario, both men are sharpened in their pastoral ministry skills, and the trainee is set up for success. This much-preferred mentoring model is marked by the following based on Philippians 2:19–24:

- **A relationship based in and built on trust** (2:19–20, 23–24). Paul trusted Timothy to represent him and care for the Philippians in the same way he would if he was there. Timothy was the next best thing to having Paul there himself. A mentor ought to be able to reproduce himself in his mentee, and a mentee ought to reflect the training and character of his mentor.

- **An unselfish spirit ought to characterize the mentor and the mentee** (2:21). Timothy prioritized the interests of Jesus Christ above his own. He got that from Paul. Likewise, a lead pastor needs to exemplify an unselfish, servant spirit that an intern or associate can emulate.

- **A mentee must be proven, just as Timothy was** (2:22a). Only experience over time can prove a person's worth in gospel ministry. Mentoring takes time—months or perhaps even years. A person's emotional, mental, and spiritual metal is tested and forged by various life experiences, such as stillbirths, sudden job losses, terminal illnesses, and divorces. Pastoring is not for the spiritual novice or the faint of heart, but for the person of God who is pursuing righteousness, godliness, faith, love, steadfastness, and gentleness (1 Timothy 6:11).

- **A father-son relationship where love and respect are expressed both ways** (2:22b). Paul was Timothy's spiritual father and perhaps more of a father to him than his own father, who was Greek and probably not a believer (Acts

16:1). A mentor is a parental figure to his mentee, someone to be trusted and loved. This indicates a level of intimacy where friendship is formed that leads to a family like relationship.

There are, no doubt, more mentoring principles to be gleaned from Paul and Timothy's relationship. Suffice it to say, however, that these four, drawn from Philippians 2:19–24, are primary and serve as a template for effective mentoring in pastoral ministry.

In my four pastorates, I purposed to give interns, assistants, and associates the opportunity to experience all that a senior pastor does for their own personal and professional enrichment. I tried not to deprive them of anything that would be for their benefit or that of the body they served. Pastoral experiences also contributed to the growth and health of my relationship with them. Accountability without looking over their shoulders is what I endeavored to practice. I was never one to micromanage or hover over them, but I tried to provide clear instructions and expectations, and then let them do it. Perhaps I gave them too much lead at times, but I preferred to err on that side versus holding the reins so tightly that they were hindered from moving forward.

Consequently, I endeavored to give them exposure to and experience in all areas of pastoral ministry. I valued their involvement both as participants and potential lead pastors. These ministry experiences included:

- Attendance and participation at weekly staff meetings, monthly leadership team meetings, and other committee meetings (i.e., missions, men's ministries, and more). I never tried to keep them from seeing pastoral ministry as a good work (1 Timothy 3:1). Being a lead pastor is hard work, but it's a good work, too. It's important that people being trained in and for pastoral ministry get a realistic exposure to it. It's not a forty-hour-a-week job; it's more like fifty-five to sixty hours a week when the time attending many meetings is included.

- Involvement in pastoral counseling sessions, such as:
  o Premarital: preparing engaged couples to be God's kind of husbands and wives.
  o Marital: serious issues, such as communication, finances, and sexual intimacy that threaten unity and intimacy.
  o Family matters: when parents and their teen children sometimes collide, or when younger children "act out," pushing parents beyond their limits of patience.
  o Crisis: the unexpected death of a child or a spouse, a sudden financial downturn, adultery, or divorce.
- Preaching: a primary part of pastoral ministry and probably the most coveted by the lead pastor. Giving up the pulpit is not easy, but it is what's best for the trainee. I tried to plan for these men to preach on Sunday mornings at least quarterly, sometimes allowing them to develop a short sermon series. I also had them preach on special occasions such as Good Friday, Mother's Day or Father's Day, Thanksgiving, or Christmas Eve. One must preach to learn how to preach. Evaluation is critical, too, as most of us of think we're better than we are, like the pastor who at Sunday dinner said to his wife proudly, "There sure are some great preachers in our day," to which she responded wryly, "Yes, but one less than you think."
- Co-officiating weddings and funerals provides valuable experiences for shepherding people during one of life's most exciting times—a wedding—to one of life's most grievous times, such as the funeral of a loved one.
- Teaching adult Bible fellowships and discipleship classes or facilitating accountability small groups. A pastor must be with his people, a principle I gleaned from Mark 3:13–14, "And he (Jesus) went up on the mountain and called to him those whom he desired, and they came to him. And

he appointed twelve (whom he also named apostles) so that they might be with him …" I tried practicing the "with him" principle throughout my pastoral ministry, seeking to invite others to be with me in various ministries.

- Attending retreats, pastors' conferences, biblical counseling training conferences, and being a server at other events. Jesus came not to be served, but to serve and to give (Matthew 20:28). Servant leadership is the best kind.
- Planning outreach events, family life seminars, or discipleship conferences and forums. Trainees need to see how these things happen from start to finish, as well as purposeful considerations.
- Visitations of various kinds, such as hospital, nursing home, funeral, and home. These are opportunities for a shepherd to be with the sheep in times of illness, grief, and on the home front.

Even though this is not an exhaustive list of local church ministries requiring pastoral oversight and pastoral involvement and personal care, it does represent necessary experiences for potential successors to experience if they are to succeed with effectiveness. Though there are variations of these pastoral duties from church to church and from staff to staff, these are transferrable to and doable by most local churches, or they are at least exemplary of what they can choose to provide.

One tendency or liability in mentoring others to succeed as lead pastors is that the lead pastor creates a clone of himself. No two people are just alike. Likewise, no two pastors are alike. It is ill-advised to try to duplicate ourselves in others. God has given each of us different abilities and temperaments, and he has given us different spiritual gifts. Common to all God-called pastors is the duty of shepherding the flock of God and taking oversight. In addressing the elders of the church in Asia Minor in the first century AD, the apostle Peter, a fellow elder, wrote, "Shepherd the flock of

God that is among you, exercising oversight, not under compulsion, but willingly, as God would have you" (1 Peter 5:2). A pastor is a shepherd.

The two men who succeeded me as lead pastors had shepherds' hearts and were leaders gifted by God to take oversight. They were similar in their strategic approach to church life and ministry and were gifted administratively. Their preaching and teaching emphasized the 2 Timothy 2:2 principle of disciples discipling disciplers. One of these men had a stronger personality than the other, but neither pastored forcefully or in an authoritarian or domineering manner. Rather, they shepherded gently and lovingly, wanting what was best for the body. One is seventeen years younger than I am, and the other is twenty-nine years my junior. In both cases, I related to these men at three different levels, depending on the situation, either as peers or protégés or prodigies. Let me address each of these "relationships," offering a brief description of each one.

- As **peers** in pastoral ministry, we often stood side by side and shoulder to shoulder in pastoral work, and I learned from them as well. I did all I could both publicly and privately to affirm them as pastors, not mere assistants to me or apprentices who would never measure up. The longer we served side by side, the more a peer relationship developed. It approached a co-pastor role and a shared ministry, according to our respective giftedness.
- As my **protégés** in pastoral ministry, I had the privilege of mentoring these men to follow me as lead pastors. It was my hope and goal for them to assume my role and, in the case of the latter, I became his associate pastor. I found that the extent to which I entrusted them with increasing pastoral oversight, the sharper their ministry skills became and the more "pastoral" or shepherd-like they became.
- As my **prodigies** in pastoral ministry, they were spiritually gifted by God to pastor or shepherd. Also, they were talented

and possessed useful skill sets. These men had what it would take to be exceptional lead pastors and, in many ways, I knew they would surpass me in ministry effectiveness. At times, I related to them as a father relates to his son, always aware they were not my actual sons, but like Timothy to Paul, beloved sons in the faith.

What a privilege it is to build relationships with people on these three different levels, yet in a complementary way. I have maintained a fast friendship with the one who is currently president of a mission agency. The seventeen-year gap in our ages lessens by the year as we have occasion to see each other several times a year. That has become a peer relationship exclusively. The other one is my pastor, and it is a privilege being shepherded by him. Though twenty-nine years younger than I, he is a fine senior pastor, leading by example and earning the trust and confidence of the people of our local assembly week by week. Although our relationship is mostly a peer relationship now, I serve somewhat as his "bench coach," and he frequently seeks my counsel and advice on pastoral matters.

The Paul-Timothy mentoring model is the preferred one. It not only prepares a person for future ministry and pastoral leadership, but is beneficial for the mentor as well as the mentee. I echo Paul's words written of Timothy, "But you know Timothy's proven worth, how as a son with a father he has served with me in the gospel" (Philippians 2:22). Paul practiced the "with me" example of Jesus Christ (Mark 3:14). There is no better model than of Jesus and his men. Clearly, Jesus was the master teacher, and the disciples were the students. But the principle recorded in Luke 6:40 is worth noting: "A disciple is not above his teacher, but everyone when he is fully trained will be like his teacher." There is no substitute for life-on-life, front-row training in pastoral ministry. There are several biblical examples of this, such as Moses and Joshua, Elijah and Elisha, and Paul and Timothy. It's the best and most-effective model for preparing people for ministry and transitions. It's biblical and what's best for the body.

9

CHAPTER

THE DISCOMFORTS OF TRANSITION

(It's Not Easy, but a Good Hard)

I t has been said that the one thing you can count on is change. Change is a part of life. Our bodies change with age; our families change in time; our jobs change—some more often than others—and leadership changes, whether in a company, in the government, or in a local church. Change happens. Some change is for better and some for worse. Some is good and some is bad, or at least not preferable. And the older we get, the harder it is to accept change. We like the familiar and find security in what we can count on. Change, even good change, is often uncomfortable and may meet with resistance.

Pastoral transitions include change, lots of change. But lest the impression is left that a pastoral transition can be done without difficulty and discomfort, let me be clear in stating that it cannot. Difficulty and discomfort are the hard realities that accompany change. Even though my experiences were good ones and preferable to other pastoral transition models, there were and will be aspects of the model I am proposing that are difficult and uncomfortable, if not awkward and downright hard. Let me explain.

As the one who willingly moved aside or stepped down as lead pastor for a younger associate to assume that role, I found some things harder to accept than others. Even though it was the right move, one that I had agreed to and had prepared for, not everything was easy. Thus, let me share some of the discomforts of pastoral transitions that should be anticipated or at least prepared for by a former lead pastor.

A lead pastor transitioning out may be marginalized during the search process and not included or consulted by the search team. That will be uncomfortable, as being kept out of the loop will be different and difficult even though it is understandable. In addition, it will be difficult at times to watch from the sidelines as decisions are made about the candidating planning and processes for both the lead and associate pastors. Once the lead pastor-elect is confirmed, it is natural for him to begin assuming his new role and responsibilities, despite the current lead pastor still holding that office.

During that two-month interim between our associate pastor being approved as the new lead pastor and then becoming effective, one caveat that softened this for me was what happened during my last leadership team meeting as the lead pastor. The lead pastor-elect had asked all the deacons to share a brief testimony of what they appreciated about me while I was the lead pastor. That was both humbling and encouraging, and very thoughtful—not to mention emotional at times. After forty years of leading deacon or trustee or leadership team meetings, I was done. The leadership baton was about to be passed. But my time leading leadership team meetings ended well with some very affirming kudos.

Another caveat was the need to develop a new rhythm of ministry as an associate pastor. For the first time in over forty years, I was preaching once every six months instead of weekly. Because preaching is a primary and regular part of a lead pastor's role, when it became only occasional for me, that was not an easy adjustment. I redesigned the priorities of my time. The whiplash effect of no longer preaching or teaching regularly was significant. One thing I did do, however, was put my name out to other local churches as a pulpit supply. Shortly after that, two pastors contacted me, and I was able to preach two Sundays in a row. That was a blessing!

Other "hard" parts of the transition included:

- Having previously been the pastor to give the first and sometimes final word on matters, letting someone else do that was difficult, especially when my counsel or decision would've been different.
- Sitting in weekly staff and pastor meetings without leading them was different. It wasn't easy being more an observer than a participant. Also, sitting in monthly leadership team meetings without moderating them was an adjustment. I was used to offering recommendations and fielding feedback. Waiting my turn was different, but not bad.
- It wasn't easy drawing the line between what to do and not to do. For example, I was accustomed to taking the lead on new projects or ministry initiatives. My role changed to giving feedback and following directives. Again, it was not wrong or bad, but it was very different and, at times, difficult.
- It was awkward becoming productive in areas of ministry I had not been given to before, but for which I was now responsible. I have good initiative and am a self-starter, so this wasn't as hard as other things I needed to adjust to. But, thinking in ways inconsistent with previous pastoral experience or responsibilities took time. I was now "second chair," and I needed to support the new lead pastor, deferring to him as the senior pastor.

I could mention other difficulties and discomforts, but I don't want to leave the impression that these outweighed the delights and pleasures. These are just some of what comes with the "transition" territory following decades of being a lead pastor and then stepping down and aside for the new lead to assert himself appropriately. Hard and difficult does not mean it was not worth it, and discomforts don't mean it isn't good or worthwhile. In the end, it's part of what

God uses in making *all* things—good and bad, easy and hard, comfortable and uncomfortable—work together for good and for what's best for the body.

I have not addressed the hard challenges or fallout that may occur when a proposed transition does not eventuate or materialize. Sometimes transitions just don't happen as envisioned or planned. Even though a transition did occur in each church I pastored, each one was different with its own challenges, and there were threats that were confronted and overcome.

One "threat" was feeling marginalized in preaching and teaching. The frequency of my preaching was dramatically decreased, and I no longer had a consistent teaching ministry. The combination of these two things was hard to accept. I dealt with this by having a one-on-one talk with the next lead pastor, explaining the need to exercise my teaching gifts and abilities more often. He received what I shared with an understanding heart and immediately made changes, giving me more opportunities to preach and teach moving forward.

But what happens when a transition does not materialize? What if the transition stalls and stops, and the lead pastor stays? What then? Presumably, there would be issues of trust, confidence, vision, or relationship to be faced and managed. How should local church leadership and congregations navigate those issues? Hopefully, church leadership will handle those prayerfully and wisely and perhaps a stronger foundation for ongoing ministry would be built. Or maybe the most effective years of pastoral ministry for the one who stays would be realized. Or Lord willing, the overall health of that local church would improve. In the wisdom of God, it could be that a "failed" transition was a success after all, in God's eyes.

Remember, the process, not the outcome, is God's goal. I raise these questions to acknowledge that transitions do not always happen, even after a carefully crafted process has been followed. Admittedly, that may *not* be what is best for the body.

10

CHAPTER

VARIATIONS OF TRANSITION MODELS
(No One Size Fits All)

The pastoral transition model that I am advocating is neither the only model nor the perfect one. It is a preferred model since, in my experience, it has proven to be the one that effectively enables a local church to transition from one pastor to another relatively seamlessly, or at least with less awkwardness and discomfort. But there are variations of this model that may be better suited for some local churches. Still, in any case, the overriding principle of what's best for the body needs to be preserved or maintained. Whatever transition method or model a local church and its leadership choose to follow or practice, the integrity and health of the congregation must be the top priority.

One variation is where the lead pastor carefully selects a person to mentor who is not currently on staff but who is brought in for that purpose. This may be necessary where none of the other people on staff are suited for or capable of becoming a lead pastor. In some cases, a successor to the lead pastor who is leaving or retiring needs to be discovered and then groomed. This discovery could be made by bringing another person on staff for a probationary period, that is, until it is determined whether or not he is a good fit as the successor to the lead pastor.

A friend of mine is the lead pastor of a large local church. He's sixty-five years old and has three younger men on staff with him, all of whom are in their twenties and early thirties and who may not have the experience or preparation necessary for succeeding him as lead pastor. I suggested to my friend, who is three to five years from retiring, that he consider calling a forty-something person with previous pastoral experience to prepare or groom as the next lead pastor. That minister would need to be presented to the church as being called for that purpose so that the other men on staff and the congregation know the plan up front. Although there are some liabilities with this model, such as the loss of a present pastor on staff who now knows he's not being considered, this is a doable model that would preserve the doctrinal integrity of the church and provide a more seasoned and mature person who has had time to get to know the congregation and vice versa before taking the lead role.

This is similar to the preferred model, which is the premise of this book. It has more risks, however, in terms of current staff longevity, but it does have the advantage of being above board and transparent about a succession plan. It allows the current lead pastor, church leadership team, ministry staff, and congregation time for observation and evaluation. No one is asked or expected to make quick decisions. A fair and comprehensive timeframe of one to two years allows for suitable decision-making on both sides.

Another model is where a person within the membership of the church is targeted at some point as having lead pastor potential because of the person's skill set and spiritual giftedness. Initially, he could be "groomed" for pastoral ministry through opportunities to preach, teach, shepherd, and administrate over the course of several years. If the church continues to affirm his potential, formal education may be offered at the graduate or seminary level, allowing him to pursue a Master of Ministry or Master of Divinity degree. This model would require "buy in" by those in leadership and consensus about his potential, not to mention his calling. An advantage is the person's extended exposure to the church and vice versa. He would be a known entity and, hopefully, would have earned the love and respect of the church family over the course of several years. A confirmation of the person's "call" would be a distinct advantage in this model.

In my current ministry, there is a young man in his early thirties who is beloved by the body. He has a secular job but invests many hours a week in local church ministries, including worship leading, audio-visual expertise, men's ministries, and youth ministry. He is a faithful man who is gifted by God for ministry. Our lead pastor meets with him regularly to mentor him and to resource him for his current ministries. He is teachable and has a submissive spirit toward authority. His wife complements him and partners with him in the worship and youth group ministries. He is also bilingual and the son of a pastor. Whether or not he will be affirmed to serve on the pastoral team someday remains to be seen. He has no formal theological education but is willing to pursue that either online or by extension. A situation like this one has real promise, and people like this man need to be cultivated for vocational ministry. It represents another variation of the proposed model of this book.

One thing common to each of these three models is the commitment by the local church congregation and leadership to nurturing and cultivating people for ministry. Mentoring and patiently grooming others for pastoral leadership is not simply based upon personality or talents or experience, but upon giftedness and the way God has equipped a person spiritually and according to God-given natural abilities that are complemented by spiritual gifts. Unfortunately, there are too many self-called people in pastoral ministry as opposed to "God-called" people, as well as those who didn't know what else to do, so they became pastors. Woe to the church that has not done its due diligence in preparing people for pastoral ministry and that is willing to settle for "good enough" rather than God's person.

In his classic book on prayer, *Power Through Prayer*, first published in 1972, E. M. Bounds wrote, "We are constantly on a stretch, if not a strain, to devise new methods, new plans, new organizations to advance the Church and secure enlargement and efficiency for the gospel. This trend of the day has a tendency to lose sight of the man or sink the man in the plan or organization. God's plan is to make much of the man, far more of him than of anything else. Men are God's method. The Church is looking for better methods; God is looking for better men" (page 5). E. M. Bounds understood the difference between methods and people and between "make do with what we have" and "wait until God sends his man to us." Spirit-led, Spirit-filled observation and a proving period is the better method—one that God blesses.

I know of a church that sacrificed waiting for God's person on the altar of "let's call the closest one at hand" or the most convenient one to call. Following a long-term pastorate that was fruitful and blessed by God, that lead pastor was called to another ministry. A seemingly promising younger man on staff gaining needed pastoral experience was still untried. The man who left did not recommend to the leadership that they consider the associate, as he needed more time to mature, but for the sake of convenience, the search committee decided to pursue this younger associate. By convenience, I mean that he was already there (i.e., he had no moving expenses), and they knew and liked him and his wife. He was a good preacher (e.g., he connected well with the younger generation), and he was younger and promised to be around a while (i.e., he had long-term potential). So, on the altar of convenience, due diligence was sacrificed. But much more than that was sacrificed.

In time, it became clear that he was not ready to be a lead pastor, but there were serious issues beneath the surface of his marriage. The fact that he and his wife were having problems became apparent, and this ultimately disqualified him. Within the first year of his ministry as lead pastor, moral issues were discovered. To counsel them toward recovery, the couple was sent away for intensive marital counseling more than once. In the end, he had to resign, which caused a sad setback in the ministry. People left the church, trust and confidence in the leadership were fractured, and the couple left more damaged than restored. This is just one tragic story of a pastoral search gone badly, but there are many more. In fact, this same church went through a similar scenario in its next search. Very sad.

So, was this avoidable? I believe so. Not because the model proposed in this book is foolproof or always guaranteed to have a good outcome, but because the model I'm suggesting, or a variation thereof, has several built-in safeguards and follows a more biblical process. E. M. Bounds words ring true: "This trend of the day has a tendency to lose sight of the man or sink the man in the plan or organization. God's plan is to make much of the man, far more of him than of anything else. Men are God's method." That was written in 1972. Was that true in 1872? How about AD 72? Will that be true in 2072, if the Lord has not returned? Yes. Yes. Yes. Yes. It has always been true and always will be if the church is on the earth and redeemed people are part of the process. Why settle for something less when we can experience so much more that is best for the body and will glorify the Lord Jesus Christ, the bridegroom and head of the church, his bride and body?

APPENDICES

APPENDIX A:
THE REST OF THE STORY
(God Does the Unexpected in Proving Preparation)

American radio broadcaster Paul Harvey was famous for his idiosyncratic delivery of news stories with dramatic pauses, cryptic comments, and standard lead-ins and sign offs. His signature sign-off was, "And now you know the rest of the story." In this chapter, I wish to tell "the rest of the story" as it relates to my transitions in more than forty-two years of pastoral ministry. It has been said that truth is stranger than fiction. In my case, what God did far exceeded anything I could have asked for or thought.

I began pastoral ministry in July 1979, having graduated from seminary the month before. A struggling Baptist church in Ohio asked me to fill the pulpit, or so I thought. It was a four-year-old church plant that had had two full time pastors and one interim. Unbeknown to me, the information I was given about the church was at least two years old. My wife, daughter, and I went there expecting to find a church of about fifty people. Instead, there were thirteen in attendance who were planning to close in September if they were unable to call a pastor. Surprisingly, the "pulpit supply" opportunity was, in reality, a candidating experience. After the evening service, the head deacon told me they had taken a vote and that it was unanimous. They wanted me to come as their pastor. My wife and I were stunned but agreed to pray about it and give them an answer later that week. Our heads were spinning and our hearts were conflicted as the need was obvious, but the offer was unexpected and the future was at risk.

Despite the admonition of one mission agency vice president who told me he would "not to touch it with a ten-foot pole," following much prayer and other counsel, I accepted the call. My wife and I, and our one-year-old daughter, moved from north central Indiana to central Ohio, assured that God had called us to this handful of hurting-but-hopeful believers. On our first Sunday morning, the three of us made sixteen in attendance. Thus, we began a pastoral ministry that lasted nearly eleven years. The church met in a rented senior citizen's center where we set up on Saturday nights and tore down on Sunday evenings. We met for worship in the main assembly area, were given a small office to use as a Sunday school classroom, and used the ante room to the ladies' restroom as the nursery. Every time a woman needed to use the restroom, the cries of babies spilled out into the "worship center." But by the grace of God, through fervent prayer and a lot of hard work, the congregation increased in number. We bought land and built a building within the first five years. By the time we moved into our new building, we were about 125 strong with a vision for reaching our community with the gospel of Jesus Christ and teaching one another the Word of God.

By 1987, the church had grown enough to consider adding an assistant pastor. That summer, David, a Christian college student, was hired for a three-month internship with an emphasis on youth ministry. Following his internship, the church voted to call him as a full-time assistant to the pastor. He was married that December, and he and his wife served faithfully for two years. In 1989, he was called to a Christian camp in northern Michigan. It was hard seeing them leave, but we all knew it was the right call, as they always had hoped to do camp ministry someday. That day had come.

Fast forward thirty years. In August 2019, the associate pastor and I were preparing and planning for his transition to lead pastor and mine to associate pastor. I suggested that he contact David, who had recently graduated from seminary. Yes, the same David who served as my first assistant thirty years previously. After twenty-six years at a Christian camp, David sensed God's leading to prepare for pastoral ministry. In 2015, he and his wife left camp ministry, and he enrolled as a student in seminary. So, thirty years following their departure from our church family in Ohio, David and his wife were waiting on the Lord for his direction for pastoral ministry. It was my hope and prayer that the Lord would direct them to where I was pastoring in Ohio.

The associate pastor who would succeed me as lead contacted David, and they began communicating about a future associate's role. This was in anticipation of my projected retirement, ensuring that there would still be two full-time pastors on staff when I retired. David accepted the call in August to come as an associate pastor.

Thirty-one years after he and I parted ministry paths and one year after being contacted, David arrived and began his ministry as associate pastor. Once again, he and I were serving side by side and shoulder to shoulder, but this time as coassociate pastors. In the words of my dear, departed dad, "Whodathunk."

In 1987, I never could have imagined that thirty-three years later, David I would be on the same pastoral team with his beginning pastoral ministry and my moving toward retirement. Then, I was thirty-five and he was twenty-two. I was cutting my teeth in my first pastoral ministry, and David was a wet-behind-the-ears summer intern in youth ministry. It was a good match, and we grew up together. Thirty-three years later, I was sixty-eight and David was fifty-five. Both of us were well-seasoned in life and ministry. In God's kindness, he brought David and me full circle. Once again, we were partnering in pastoral ministry. It was new, but familiar. It was different, but similar.

God said in Isaiah 55:8–9: "For my thoughts are not your thoughts, neither are your ways my ways, declares the LORD. For as the heavens are higher than the earth, so are my ways higher than your ways and my thoughts than your thoughts." Although these verses speak of a different time and people, it is the same LORD and the same truth. I could neither have anticipated nor scripted what God did. The two years that David and I had together in Ohio were in preparation for the two years we would have together prior to my retirement. David was a good complement to me in my first pastorate in Delaware, Ohio in 1987, and he has proven to be the same for the new lead pastor of Shawnee Hills Baptist Church in Jamestown, Ohio presently.

And now you know the rest of the story. It's a true story that reads like fiction. It's a real story that stretches the imagination. It's a beautiful story of the providential work of God in preparing lives, arranging ministries, and aligning giftedness to provide effective local church ministry and to do what's best for the body.

The biblical principle illustrated by this is that preparation for effective ministry takes time. Joseph was thirteen years into being prepared by God to become second in command to Pharaoh of Egypt when severe famine ravaged Egypt and the surrounding nations. Moses was eighty years old before he became the lawgiver and deliverer of Israel, "going to school" for forty years in Egypt as royalty and then another forty years in the wilderness as a shepherd. Paul was in training for seventeen years before becoming the apostle of apostles. Jesus lived in obscurity for thirty years before beginning his public ministry. God never hurries the process of preparing people for ministry, for the process itself is the goal.

Care must be given to following a process that may take longer than anticipated. Patience in a process is needed since most worthwhile things usually come slowly. By definition, a process is a series of progressive and interdependent steps by which an end is attained. Preparation is the action or process of making something ready for use or service, or of getting ready for some occasion. In the thirty years preceding his public ministry, Jesus "increased in wisdom and in stature and in favor with God and man" (Luke 2:52). God knows what He's about in preparing men and local churches, for ministry and transitions in ministry.

When God wants to drill a man
And thrill a man
And skill a man
When God wants to mold a man to play the noblest part.
When He yearns with all His heart to create so great and bold a man
That all the world shall be amazed,
Watch His methods, watch His ways …
God knows what He's about.
—Anonymous

APPENDIX B:
TRANSITIONS AND CHANGE
(New Leader, Same Lord)
Joshua 1 (Part 1)

It has been said, "There is nothing more permanent than that which is temporary." Although what was meant to be temporary can become permanent, sooner or later everything changes. Change is a part of life. You can count on it. Children grow up, parents grow old, jobs change, teens go to college, twenty-somethings graduate, singles get married, and friends and relatives move or die. Change happens. But God doesn't change, and neither does his Word. Still, God uses change to train us to trust him and to grow us.

Moses' life changed dramatically over his 120 years—from being in the household of Pharaoh for the first forty years of his life, to being an outcast desert shepherd until he was eighty, to being chosen by God to deliver Israel from the bondage of Egypt. From the exodus of Egypt through the wilderness wanderings, Moses, the servant of the Lord, led the people of God. He was their deliverer and lawgiver, God's prophet. But after forty years of wilderness wandering, the generation that left Egypt, including Moses, was dead. A new generation had grown up who would have a new leader to take them into the long-awaited Promised Land. This was all part of God's plan for expanding his influence and showing his glory. The God who doesn't change used major transitions and change to reveal his power and faithfulness, and to fulfill his promises to Abraham, Isaac, and Jacob.

As the book of Joshua begins, Israel's wanderings are over, Moses is dead, and Joshua is the new leader. Israel is encamped east of the Jordan River, poised to enter Canaan (Joshua 1:1–2). God's people needed to get up and get going! It was time to cross the Jordan River and occupy the land God gave them (verse 2). Leadership transitions and change characterize how God develops and grows his people, accomplishing his work and will. Change can be unsettling, uncomfortable, and fearful. Unknowns and uncertainties accompany change, even when they're expected. Imagine what the Israelites were thinking as they awaited the next step—entrance into Canaan. They had been anticipating this moment for forty years. Now it was here, but how?

In Joshua 1, God reveals truths that transcend historical and cultural contexts. There are transitions in pastorates and changes in ministries, but God and his Word do not change. So, what should we embrace that was true 2,500 years ago or longer that was and always will be true?

First, God is unchanging. He's perfectly consistent in character and conduct. Moses wrote of the eternal, unchanging God, "From everlasting to everlasting, you are God" (Psalm 90:1–2). David wrote of the immutable God, "He only is my rock and my salvation, my fortress; I shall not be greatly shaken" (Psalm 62:2). God said of himself, "For I the LORD do not change" (Malachi 3:6). In the book of Hebrews we read, "Jesus Christ is the same yesterday and today and forever" (Hebrews 13:8). In the changing circumstances of our local churches, we worship and serve a changeless God. He is our Rock and our Redeemer.

Second, God is faithful and true. His people can always take him at his word. His mercies or covenant loyalties are new each morning. Great is his faithfulness! Like God's people of old, we can count on him for the following:

- A plan that will work. He always knows what to do and how and when to do it. He knows the outcome of the process we're following.
- Godly, Spirit-filled leadership. He prepares the right people for the right times. We can trust him to do that.
- A process that is purposeful and effective. The process itself is the goal more than the outcome. We must not miss what he's up to.
- Providing what is needed when it is needed. He provided a leader, land, resources, and rest for Israel. He will provide for our needs.
- Keeping his promises. He is true to his word and cannot lie. We can trust him because he is true and trustworthy.

Like the demonized boy's father whom Jesus encouraged to trust him, we may say, "Lord, I believe; help my unbelief." Sometimes we want to trust him because we're not sure how it's all going to work out. But, if we knew how, we wouldn't need faith.

Third, God's glory is the main thing. Though he gives generously, loves lavishly, and will not withhold good from those who walk uprightly, he will not share his glory. Glory is God's alone. God is jealous of his glory. Moses learned that the hard way when he struck the rock instead of speaking to it. The people of Israel saw an angry man, not the glory of God. Thus, he was not allowed to enter Canaan. We must glorify God in this time of transition and change. His ways are not our ways, neither are his thoughts our thoughts. They are much higher and better. To God be the glory!

In this season of pastoral leadership transitions and anticipated changes, we can feel unsettled and have many questions. But God and his Word haven't changed and neither has our mission. We must trust in the Lord, waiting patiently on him to provide the right leadership at the right time. God knows what we need. Here are four assurances or truths we can count on:

- As God was with Moses and Joshua, so he is with us (Joshua 1:5).
- As God promised neither to leave nor forsake Israel, so he will neither leave nor forsake us (Joshua 1:5).
- As Israel had his word and committed to obeying him, so we have the same Word and must choose to obey (Joshua 1:8, 17).
- As Joshua was exhorted to be strong and courageous, so we are to be strong and courageous and not be frightened or dismayed (Joshua 1:7, 9, 18).

From where comes the courage and strength to do what God wants? Our help comes from the Lord, the maker of heaven and earth (Psalm 122:1). How was that infused into the life of Joshua and the people of Israel? By the Word of God, that is, the voice of truth (Joshua 1:6–7). In Joshua 1, the plan was communicated (vv. 2–4), victory was guaranteed (vv. 1:5a, 7b), and God's presence was assured (vv. 1:5b, 9). He will be with us, too. He gives the assignment, provides the resources, and then stays with his people. He's the God who stays. He will never leave us or forsake us. We have his word on that (Hebrews 13:8), and his Word cannot be broken (John 10:35). This always will be what's best for the body.

TRANSITIONS AND CHANGE
(The Lord Speaks)
Joshua 1 (Part 2)

In the *Mission Impossible* action movies, mission commander Swanbeck gives assignments to agent Ethan Hunt by prerecorded messages: "Good morning, Mr. Hunt. Your mission, should you choose to accept it, involves _____. You may select any team members. As always, should you or any member of your team be caught or killed, the secretary will disavow all knowledge of your actions. This message will self-destruct in five seconds." These assignments were dangerous and seemingly impossible. But incredible resources were at Ethan Hunt's disposal for the success of these "impossible" missions.

Joshua and the people of Israel were given a "mission impossible" of their own, forty years after the exodus from Egypt. Two to three million people were encamped east of the Jordan River that separated them from the Promised Land. Even if they could cross the Jordan (there were no bridges or ferries), they still had to face the Canaanites, the fearful and idolatrous inhabitants of the land. But the God who delivered them by the hand of Moses from Egypt, opened the Red Sea for them to cross on dry ground, and preserved them in the wilderness by feeding them manna and quail and kept their sandals and clothes from wearing out, spoke to Joshua. Thankfully, the words of Jehovah did not self-destruct. They are preserved as part of the Old Testament scriptures for our encouragement and hope (Joshua 1:2–9; Romans 15:4).

God guaranteed their forefathers the success of Israel's mission to enter, conquer, and possess Canaan, but daunting challenges and obstacles awaited them. They would need to take God at his Word, trusting him to lead them to victory and not defeat. Remember, the previous generation did not take God at his Word. Though the land was everything and more than they had expected, the giants in the land were too imposing of a threat. The people backed off, refusing to follow their leadership which had encouraged them to trust in the Lord and take the land.

Following Moses as the leader of Israel into Canaan was overwhelming. Mission impossible? Not when following the one with whom all things are possible. But it was daunting enough for God to say to Joshua, "Do not be frightened and do not be dismayed" (Joshua 1:9). Thus, three times, God exhorted him to be strong and courageous (Joshua 1:6, 7, 9). Is courage the absence of fear? No, but it is the opposite of cowardice or the spirit that withdraws from the dangers and difficulties that come with doing the will of God (2 Timothy 1:7). Courage is that quality of mind that enables people to encounter danger and difficulty with firmness and resolve, despite inner fears. The great reformer, Martin Luther, feared people so little because he feared God so much. When he set out on his momentous journey to Worms, he said, "You can expect from me everything save fear and recantation. I shall not flee, much less recant." When warned of the grave dangers, he retorted, "Not go to Worms? I shall go to Worms though there were as many devils as tiles on the roofs."

In times of transition and change, what was true for Joshua and Israel is true for God's people today. From where does the courage and strength come to do what God wants us to do? God himself. But how does he convey this to his people? How was that infused into the life of Joshua and then into Israel? It came by the Word of God (Joshua 1:6–7). By God's spoken word the plan was communicated (1:2–4), victory was guaranteed (1:5a, 7b), and God's presence was assured (1:5b, 9). He would be with Joshua and Israel (1:5–6). Commander Swanbeck never promised to be with Ethan Hunt. He simply gave him the assignment, provided the resources, and sent him to do or die. God is the perfect commander. He gives the assignment, provides the resources, and stays with his people at all times. In Acts 18:9–10, Jesus spoke in a night vision to a fearful Paul in Corinth and said, "Do not be afraid, but go on speaking and do not be silent, for I am with you, and no one will attack you to harm you, for I have many in this city who are my people." Consequently, Paul stayed another eighteen months teaching the Word of God. Jesus' words emboldened Paul to teach God's Word despite obstacles.

But God uses obstacles to prove his sufficiency, build courage, and increase strength in his people. There were three obstacles that stood between Joshua, Israel, and the Promised Land:

- The Jordan River (Joshua 1:2, "go over this Jordan"). It is likely the river was at flood stage at that time of year and had overflowed its banks.
- The Canaanites in the land (Joshua 1:2–4). This was hostile territory. The Canaanites consisted of different ethnic groups who would not welcome them. There would be resistance, and battles were certain.
- The people of Israel (Joshua 1:2, "all this people"). They were two to three million strong with a reputation for being stubborn and rebellious, and it was a mixed multitude consisting of Israelites and Egyptians.

Unbelief and lack of courage prevented Israel from entering the land forty years before. Joshua needed to act on God's Word and rely on God's presence, promises, and provision—and then lead.

What are the obstacles before us in this time of transition? Not a river, but a transition period involving adjustments by the leadership team, ministry staff, and each member of the body. Not Canaanites and walled cities, but unknowns, adjustments, and opportunities. God wants us to move ahead and trust him, but we don't know all that lies ahead. Our faith will be tested. We, ourselves, can be obstacles. We are both assets and liabilities. We can be our own worst enemies if we are not trusting God, obeying his Word, and relying on God-given resources and leadership.

In Joshua 1:7–8, God's guarantee of prosperity and good success for Joshua is recorded. Then in verse 1:9a, there is the reminder of who's in charge. God had them in a process that, though programmed for success, included obstacles and a threefold warning:

- Be careful! There were dangers, so be wise and alert. Guaranteed success was no excuse for being caught off guard. How? Speak and talk about the Word of God. Be doers of the Word!
- Be committed! Give heed to the whole counsel of God (Acts 20:31–32). Think God's thoughts consistently and walk carefully and wisely. Be people of prayer!
- Be Christ-conscious! Stay on task and avoid distractions and detours (Joshua 1:7b). They needed to conduct their lives in obedience to all God's commands. So do we. We are to be imitators of Christ!

Even though God had given them the land, they had to enter, conquer, and occupy. They needed to trust and obey. So do we.

Mission possible is before us, and we have God's Word on this. God knows the outcome and what it will look like moving forward. Let's practice Proverbs 3:5–6 together. We must trust, lean not, and acknowledge!

TRANSITIONS AND CHANGE

(The Leader Speaks)
Joshua 1 (Part 3)

On August 28, 1963, on the steps of the Lincoln Memorial, a thirty-four-year-old black Baptist clergyman, who was an activist in the civil rights movement, stood before a throng of people gathered in the mall. There, the renowned "I Have a Dream" speech was delivered by Dr. Martin Luther King Jr. This is a classic example of a person's vision being clearly articulated with passion. No one doubted what was in his heart or what he believed. He gave voice to a vision, and people followed him. That's a leader. In the heart of a true leader, there is a vision of what he or she believes must be, can be, and will be. A leader with a clear vision shared passionately will have a following.

But when that vision comes from God and is communicated with confidence in God, the vision-giver, others will put confidence and trust in that leader. Joshua was God's kind of leader. The Lord spoke to him and gave him the vision of conquering and occupying the land promised to his forefathers. To realize that vision, Israel needed to act on it by crossing the Jordan River into Canaan, which was no small feat. God promised that he would provide for them and be with them always. The same Lord who was with Moses and who spoke to Joshua, their new leader, then spoke to the people of Israel (Joshua 1:10–15). The vision was conceived by God in Joshua's heart, who cast it. The people caught it and committed to following their leader and the Lord. In Joshua 1:10–15, the leader speaks, commanding the officers to command the people. Joshua acted promptly, showing confidence in the Lord and the courage needed to tackle the task. In God's work, there is a chain of command:

- God is the commander in chief: "Have not I commanded ..."
- God's leaders obey his commands before commanding others.
- God's people commit to following leaders who follow the Lord.

God is trustworthy and leads his people through trustworthy leaders. The "officers" were actually scribes in charge of enrollment. Their responsibility was to keep accurate registers of the people according to tribes and families. When orders were issued for public work or military service, the scribes communicated these to all the tribes. In these verses are two commands to obey.

The command to prepare (1:10–11): "Get ready to go!" The people were commanded to prepare food supplies to sustain them in the early days of being in the land. In just three days, they would be in Canaan, but they were encamped eight miles east of the Jordan. Picture this: three million people and their stuff, stretched a mile wide and sixteen miles long. At a speed of two miles per hour, it would take them four hours to get to the Jordan before crossing it.

The first step of their mission was to cross over the Jordan River. It was harvest time, and the banks of the Jordan were flooded. Normally, the Jordan was one hundred feet across and three to seventeen feet deep. At flood stage, it would've been much wider since its banks overflowed and the river was deeper and swifter. How were they to cross? They weren't ordered to build rafts or a bridge. Neither were they asked to vote on the plan. They were simply to obey the commands and follow their leader to whom God had spoken. God had a plan.

Preparation is essential for progress. Much preparation has preceded our current transition process. We don't need food supplies for the days ahead, but we do need to be well-prepared. In planning to be ready, we will need the teaching and preaching of God's Word. Why? So, when the time comes, we'll be ready to move ahead. God's word to us is, "Be ready to move ahead!" But there is a second command.

The command to partner (1:12–15): "Help the rest before you rest!" The tribes of Reuben, Gad, and half of Manasseh requested to settle on land east of the Jordan. But they were commanded to help conquer the land with the other tribes before settling down (Numbers 32:1–33). Why? So as not to discourage the others (Joshua 1:6-13, 20-23). These two and a half tribes would be the advance troops, "the men of valor … armed," constituting five companies of courageous warriors who would prepare the way for the rest. What valuable partners they were to the other nine-and-a-half tribes. It was vital that *all* the tribes participated in conquering the land. Each person was needed with each one needing to do his or her part. This was a twelve-tribe or all-in effort. All-in participation by a local church body is essential to realize the full benefits of serving the Lord. In some local churches, 20 percent of the membership does 80 percent of the ministry. Local church ministry is not a spectator sport. We need every member serving the Lord and one another in either adult, teen, or children's ministries. When each person does something, all of us will have ownership and share in the blessings. We are to participate individually while doing what's best for the body. How? By attending regularly, serving joyfully, praying ceaselessly, giving generously, and sharing selflessly. That's body life at its best!

A spiritual leader is one who commands respect through exercising godly, Spirit-filled authority or influence. He has followers who are motivated by his vision and want buy-in. When Israel was about to enter Canaan, they rallied around their new leader, Joshua. God spoke to Joshua, who then commanded the officers who gave orders to the people about their preparation and participation. Would Israel be faithful or rebel against their leadership? Would they trust their new leader and follow his orders? The two-and-a-half tribes of Israel represented all twelve tribes that would "do all that was commanded of them and to go wherever they were sent." Just as they respected Moses and followed him, so they would Joshua. The people's commitment to follow their new leader is declared in Joshua 1:17–18. To Joshua, the commitment was, "Only may the LORD your God be with you!" To one another, it was implied that rebels against the Lord's leader would die. Again to Joshua, it was, "Only be strong and courageous!" In any successful endeavor of God's people, the leaders must obey the Lord to earn the trust and support of the people. We will experience prosperity and success in our work and ministries as we follow the Lord and those he has placed in leadership over us.

In this time of leadership and ministry transitions, there will be more changes. Not all of them will be comfortable, but God uses transitions and change to grow us stronger and to make us more courageous. Let's give heed to the Lord's words to Joshua knowing that its application is for us, too: "Only be strong and very courageous … Do not be frightened and do not be dismayed, for the LORD your God is with you wherever you go" (Joshua 1:7, 9).

APPENDIX C:
3M COMMUNITY
PHILIPPIANS 2:1–5
(Preached the Sunday Before Voting on Lead Pastor)
April 26, 2020

The COVID-19 pandemic caused sheltering and social distancing, but unity was being cultivated through distance socializing via email, video, text, phone, and prayer. Though we were unable to gather together, there's still a blessed unity within our community. David wrote, "Behold, how good and pleasant it is when brothers dwell together in unity" (Psalm 133:1). How true and how kind of the Lord to give this to us.

It was not so in the church of Philippi. In writing to them, Paul remembered them with thanksgiving, prayed for them with joy, and regarded them as partners in the gospel and partakers of grace. But something was causing disunity in the community. Paul wrote "to all the saints in Christ Jesus" (Philippians 1:1), urging them to live worthy of the gospel of Christ (1:27–30), and stressing unity in the face of outside pressures or problems (3:2). He also urged them toward unity in the face of internal problems (4:2). Unity is vital to community. So, in Philippians 2:1–5, we find 3M CommUnity.

The motives for CommUnity (1). The word *so* links this with Philippians 1:27–30. Lives worthy of the gospel of Christ stand strong and struggle well together, even when physically apart. Body life that is a credit to God's gospel is described in Philippians 2:1–4. *If* does not convey uncertainty or doubt, but rather assumes truth and could be rendered *since*. It introduces four motives for unity.

1. Consolation in Christ. This is the encouragement that comes through comfort, which is "in Christ."
2. Comfort from (the) love (of Christ). This is the love that floods the hearts of believers providing this comfort or intimacy.
3. Communion in the (Holy) Spirit. True fellowship is forged by the Holy Spirit (of Christ).
4. Compassion (of Christ). This is affection or tenderness and sympathy or mercies, which are the very expressions of compassion.

These motives are essential, not optional. Jesus prayed for oneness or unity in John 17:20–23. By our unity, some in our respective communities will know and believe that the Father sent the Son. Although we are to be of the same mind for the sake of harmony in the body, unity has only one explanation: God sent his Son. Unity gives gospel opportunity, and we experience blessed consolation, comfort, communion, and compassion.

The mark of CommUnity (2). Paul's command is at the heart of his personal appeal for unity. What marks biblical unity? "Being of the same mind" or being likeminded. Paul called the church to focus on what they had in common and on their relationship bound up together with him. Unity is having the same love, being in full accord, and (being) of one mind. We have seen an increase of these while "staying at home." It's as if Paul were saying, "Live together in harmony and in love as if you only had one mind and one spirit between you." Doctrinal agreement is necessary for biblical unity within a local church. We must agree on the fundamentals of the faith: the virgin birth and deity of Jesus Christ, the inerrancy of scripture, the blood atonement of Christ, and his literal resurrection and second coming.

But unity is not uniformity. A wide diversity of gifts, abilities, perspectives, and opinions is found in the body of Christ. God never intended for us to look alike, dress alike, or act alike. We won't see eye to eye on everything. Diversity is a strength, not a weakness or a threat. Unity allows for disagreement without being disagreeable and divisive. The joy Paul spoke of in Philippians 1:4 was real, but incomplete. He wanted there to be room only for joy in his thoughts of them. If only they were of the same mind, then his joy would be complete. Can we be unified and live in harmony? God has saved and sanctified us for that. We are one in Christ. But how?

The means of CommUnity (Philippians 1:3–4). Humility characterizes true unity, which was personified in Christ, our perfect role model (1:3, 1:6–8). Christlike humility sets pride aside, putting others first. What is it? Humility is the absence of rivalry, selfishness, and conceit or pride (1:3a). Rivalry is selfish ambition or love of prestige. Conceit is vanity or pride. Coupled together, these represent the kind of individualism that wrecks unity. Pride pursues selfish, "me-centered" agendas. This attitude is divisive and destroys unity. Humility is the presence of lowliness, a servant's spirit. It shows:

- Consideration, "count others more significant than yourselves." Humility values others, preferring or honoring others in love.
- Concern, "look not only to your own interests, but also to the interests of others." Concern takes a good look at the needs and interests of others and does something about it. It extends a hand, saying, "What can I do to help?"

This is so Christlike. Paul wrote, "Have this mind (attitude) among yourselves, which is yours in Christ Jesus" (Philippians 2:5). Jesus said, "for I am meek and lowly in heart" and he lived it out, all the way to the cross (Matthew 11:28–30; Philippians 2:6–8). Humility seeks to serve, not to be served (Matthew 20:28). It's the antithesis of pride and selfishness and is the right attitude for prompting unity within the community. What can we do to promote harmony, like-mindedness, and unity? Individually, we need to think "others," not "I." We need to think: "What's best for the body of SHBC?" and "How do we eagerly maintain the unity of the Spirit in the bond of peace?" In other words, we need to think like Jesus! We need to have the mind or attitude of Christ. We are a community of believers who build community even from a distance by having the mind or attitude of Jesus Christ. May this mind be in you and me.

APPENDIX D:
HEART-TO-HEART
LESSONS LEARNED IN FORTY-ONE
YEARS AS A LEAD PASTOR
(Last Message as a Lead Pastor)
May 31, 2020

I became lead pastor 2,608 days ago. Tomorrow, I will become the associate pastor, the completion of a transition anticipated for over seven years. It's time for it to happen. We're ready, and it's what's best for this body moving forward. Please turn to John 3, where we read of the transition of John the baptizer to Jesus the Messiah recorded in verses 27–30: "John answered, 'A person cannot receive even one thing unless it is given him from heaven. You yourselves bear me witness, that I said, "I am not the Christ, but I have been sent before him." The one who has the bride is the bridegroom. The friend of the bridegroom, who stands and hears him, rejoices greatly at the bridegroom's voice. Therefore, this joy of mine is now complete. He must increase and I must decrease."

John compared himself to the friend of the bridegroom, or the best man, and Jesus to the bridegroom. Although this was a unique transition, there are some interesting similarities to our transition. When it was time for John to step aside, he said, "Therefore this joy of mine is now complete. He must increase and I must decrease"

(John 3:29c–30). John's mission was accomplished. It was time for him to step back and Jesus to step forward.

That's how I feel. The transition process is now complete, and I must decrease. I will follow the lead of our new lead pastor. This is my joy! By the grace of God, what was seven years in the making has now materialized. Also, God has given me the privilege of concluding forty years of lead pastor ministry with you. God is good all the time.

I would like to speak heart-to-heart, sharing a few of the lessons I've learned in the past forty years as a lead pastor and how the great shepherd has shepherded me. What I've learned about being a pastor over the past forty years can be summarized by these four lessons:

1. Preach the Word and love the people. A seasoned saint and church planter shared that principle with me as I began my first pastorate. He told me it's the best thing a pastor can do for the flock of God. I've never forgotten that godly, sage advice. It has proven to be true here as well as in the other three churches I've had the privilege of pastoring. These two practices are the priorities in pastoral ministry from which flow everything else a pastor does.

2. Slow growth is sure growth, spiritually and numerically. My wife's first pastor shared this with me in my first year as a pastor. He also said to me, "David, never aspire to be the fastest growing church in town." What's implied by this statement is that fast growth can lead to dramatic decline. Pastoral ministry is not about big budgets, more buildings, and widespread notoriety. Pastors are shepherds, not CEOs or celebrities. In addition, good growth is the outcome of discipling God's people to be spiritually healthy and growing. Healthy sheep reproduce. Maturing believers share the gospel with others, some of whom will be saved.

3. People don't care how much you know until they know how much you care. This may be cliché, but it's true. My

favorite professors in seminary were those who pastored before they taught. They had spent time with the sheep in the trenches and on the front line of ministry. Their teaching was practical, not theoretical; firsthand, not secondhand. The one exception was Dr. John C. Whitcomb, who had a God-given pastor's heart, even though he never pastored a local church. Acts of pastoral care are remembered more than your best sermons. Early morning hospital calls before a surgery, being there when a loved one dies, or listening to a crisis call at 1:00 a.m. means more than a month of messages. A good shepherd knows the sheep because he's with the sheep in good and hard times. Pastoral distancing is neither effective nor memorable.

4. Do what's best for the body of believers, not just what pleases or appeases one or two members. The body has many members and the best decisions made are with the whole church body in mind. Pastors are there to care for, not cater to the people. Pastors are there to encourage and edify, not to enable those under their care. God called me to be a pastor, despite same disappointments and sorrows, it has been a great joy. Paul wrote, "He who calls you is faithful; he will surely do it" (1 Thessalonians 5:24).

In addition to what I learned about being a pastor, I also learned lessons of how Jesus, the good and great shepherd of his sheep, shepherded or pastored me. These can be summarized in six personal statements:

1. Jehovah-Jesus loves me more than I will ever know. Despite my many mistakes, sins, and struggles, his everlasting, unconditional love has granted me forgiveness whenever I have confessed my sins. He has always been faithful to forgive me and to cleanse me from all unrighteousness (1 John 1:9).

2. Jehovah-Jesus is for me more than I will ever deserve. If he is for me, who can be against me (Romans 8:31)? When, as a thirty-five-year-old pastor, a husband of nine years, and a father of four young children, I faced the greatest crisis of my life, Jesus was for me and strengthened me.

3. Jehovah-Jesus is committed to me more than I am to him. He's a friend closer than a brother. He's been faithful when I wasn't. He faithfully shepherded my children under the pressures of being a pastor's kids growing up by saving them and safeguarding their hearts. When I unconsciously put pressure on them to live up to a certain standard or hold in confidence things that happened in our home about which they were not permitted to speak, God was faithful and good.

4. Jehovah-Jesus is my example more than anyone else. I've had good, godly role models: my dad and my two adopted dads. But Jesus is the perfect example who never fails and who showed me what to do or how to respond when at a loss. It was Jesus who taught me that when I didn't know what to do, I should do what I already knew to do. He knows what to do, so I can trust him at all times.

5. Jehovah-Jesus is my chief Shepherd, but my wife, Carolyn, is his assistant shepherd in my life. While pastoring in Pennsylvania, a man was saved in his fifties and shortly thereafter was diagnosed with bladder cancer. His family had attended church for years before he was saved. I had called on him and visited him in the hospital because I cared for him and his family. One rainy evening, he showed up unannounced on our front porch. As I opened the door and greeted him, he said, "Hi, Pastor. May I ask you a question?" I replied, "Of course." With tears in his eyes, he asked, "Pastor, you care for and pastor the members of our church, but who pastors you? Who pastors the pastors?" I was speechless, as I'd never been asked that question before, let alone by a new believer. After a long pause, I said, "Jesus

does, and he uses Carolyn to help him." That seemed to satisfy him. He thanked me and left.

6. Jehovah-Jesus loves and disciplines me for my own good but more so for his own glory. God's goal for my life and the lives of all believers is stated in Romans 8:29, "to be conformed to the image of his Son." To be like Jesus, our Father disciplines his children out of love for their own good. In Psalm 119, the psalmist wrote of the purpose and benefits of affliction: "Before I was afflicted, I went astray, but now I keep your word" (Psalm 119:67). "It is good for me that I was afflicted, that I might learn your statutes" (Psalm 119:71). "I know, O Lord, that your rules are righteous, and that in faithfulness you have afflicted me" (Psalm 119:75).

Afflictions and sufferings are used by God to build endurance, character, and hope (Romans 5:3–5). They're also allowed for the purpose of comforting others who are afflicted and suffering (2 Corinthians 1:3–7). Forty years ago, I was untested and spiritually immature. For my own good, but more for his own glory, God lovingly disciplined me to make me more like Jesus. We read of Jesus in Hebrews 5:8, "Although he was a son, he learned obedience through what he suffered."

Alan Redpath was a British evangelist, pastor, and author of the twentieth century, and who also pastored Moody Church in Chicago, Illinois, from 1953 to 1962. He has been credited with the following poignant statement:

> There is nothing—no circumstance, no trouble, no testing—than can ever touch me until first of all it has gone past God, past Christ, right through to me. If it has come that far, it has come with a great purpose, which I may not understand at the moment. But as I refuse to become panicky, as I lift

> my eyes to Him and accept it as coming from the
> throne of God for some great purpose of blessing to
> my own heart, no sorrow will disturb me, no trial
> will ever disarm me, no circumstance will cause me
> to fret for I shall rest in the joy of what my Lord is.
> This is the rest of victory.

Anything that touches my life or the life of any child of God must first pass through the strong hands of the all-wise and loving good shepherd, who is the door of his sheep. He voluntarily laid down his life and then supernaturally took up his life for the sheep (John 10:7–18).

God has allowed a variety of trials in my family to make us better, not bitter, and stronger not weaker: Our youngest daughter's congenital heart defect, the trials of being a young pastor and those that encompassed more than forty years of pastoral experience, the unexpected and difficult crises as president of a mission organization that collapsed, our son's cancer, and the diagnosis of my advanced prostate cancer and subsequent surgery, were all meant for our good. His grace is sufficient, and his power and strength are made perfect in weakness (2 Corinthians 12:9).

Believers are victors, not victims. Victims focus on how others mistreat them. Victors focus on how well they treat others. The apostle Paul wrote in 1 Corinthians 15:56–58, "The sting of death is sin, and the power of sin is the law. But thanks be to God, who gives us the victory through our Lord Jesus Christ. Therefore, my beloved brothers, be steadfast, immovable, always abounding in the work of the Lord, knowing that in the Lord your labor is not in vain." But by the grace of God, I am what I am (1 Corinthians 15:10). Furthermore, I am living in victory, which is not freedom from fighting the good fight or fatigue in the face of trials. It is a rest and being safe and secure in Christ—forever. Praise God from whom all blessings flow!

A pastor's effectiveness is dependent to a large extent upon those he pastors "standing firm in one spirit, with one mind striving together side by side for the faith of the gospel" (Philippians 1:27). Following these words, Paul wrote the following: "So, if there is any encouragement in Christ, any comfort from love, any participation in the Spirit, any affection and sympathy, complete my joy by being of the same mind having the same love, being in full accord and of one mind. Do nothing from selfish ambition or conceit, but in humility count others more significant than yourselves. Let each of you look not only to his own interests, but also to the interests of others. Have this mind among yourselves, which is yours in Christ Jesus" (Philippians 2:1-5).

For local churches that anticipate, plan, prepare for, and pray about changes and transitions in pastoral leadership, the best is yet to come. What a privilege it is to be part of what God does that is what's best for the body. To God be the glory for the great things he has done, is doing, and is yet do in the global church that is represented by local churches like ours!

BIBLIOGRAPHY

Bounds, E. M. 1972. *Power Through Prayer*. Grand Rapids, MI:
    Baker Book House

Chambers, Oswald. 1982. *My Utmost for His Highest*. Nashville,
    TN: Discovery House Publications

Scott, Stuart. 2019. *31 Ways to be A "One Another" Christian*.
    Wapwallopen, PA: Shepherd Press

Southerland, Dan. 1999. *Transitioning: Leading Your Church
    Through Change*. Grand Rapids, MI: Zondervan

Spurgeon, Charles. 1980. *Morning and Evening*. Grand Rapids,
    MI: The Zondervan Corporation

Toler, Stan. 2010. *Practical Guide for Ministry Transition*.
    Indianapolis, IN: Wesleyan Publishing House

Welch, Edward T. 2018. *Caring for One Another*. Wheaton,
    Illinois: Crossway

AZ Quotes. Philip Melancthon Quotes. www.azquotes.com/
    author/27811-Philip_Melancthon

Quotes of Famous People. Charles Wesley about John Wesley.
    https://quotepark.com/quotes/1776007-john-wesley-god-bur
    ies-his-workmen-but-carries-on-his-work/

Printed in the United States
by Baker & Taylor Publisher Services